NAVIGATE 2.0

NAVIGATE 2.0
SELLING THE WAY PEOPLE LIKE TO BUY

DUSTIN HILLIS
and
STEVE REINER

A Southwestern Consulting Book
Published by Southwestern Consulting
Southwestern/Great American, Inc.
2451 Atrium Way, Nashville, TN 37214

Southwesternconsulting.com
Part of the Southwestern Family of Companies

NAVIGATE 2.0: SELLING THE WAY PEOPLE LIKE TO BUY

Copyright © 2016 by Southwestern Consulting

Southwestern Consulting supports copyright. Copyright fuels creativity, encourages diverse voices, promotes free speech, and creates a vibrant culture. Thank you for buying an authorized edition of this book and for complying with copyright laws by not reproducing, scanning, or distributing any part of it in any form without permission. You are supporting writers and allowing Southwestern Consulting to continue to publish books for readers.

10 9 8 7 6 5

PRODUCED IN THE UNITED STATES OF AMERICA

Project management by Author Bridge Media, www.AuthorBridgeMedia.com:
Project manager and editor in chief: Helen Chang
Editor: Kristine Serio
Publishing manager: Laurie Aranda
Cover design: Derek Britton
Interior design: Author Bridge Media, www.AuthorBridgeMedia.com
Illustrator: Tristan McNatt, Nashville, TN

Dustin Hillis Photo © Marisa McKaye

Library of Congress Number: 2016914578
ISBN: 978-0-9815657-3-6 - Hardcover
978-0-9815657-4-3 - Softcover
978-0-9815657-5-0 - Ebook
978-0-9815657-6-7 - Audiobook

While the authors have made every effort to provide accurate information at the time of publication, neither the publisher nor the authors assume any responsibility for errors, or for changes that occur after publication. Further, the publisher does not have any control over and does not assume any responsibility for authors or third-party websites or their content.

Most Southwestern Consulting books are available at special quantity discounts for bulk purchases for sales promotions, premiums, fundraising, or educational use. Special books, or book excerpts, can be created to fit specific needs at the compliance of the authors.

For details, write info@southwesternconsulting.com

TESTIMONIALS

"Dustin Hillis and Steve Reiner do a phenomenal job of taking complicated behavior science and making it easy to understand and, even more importantly, implementing it for today's sales professional. *Navigate 2.0* is a must-read for any salesperson wanting to turn professional."

—**Ron Marks,** *Amazon bestselling author of* **Managing for Sales Results**

"This book is fantastic! Hillis and Reiner's ideas are believable and easy to understand. The beginning salesperson will start on a solid foundation. The veteran salesperson will discover new ideas that will lift him or her to new heights of excellence."

—**Steve Savage,** *coauthor of* **Guerrilla Business Secrets** *with Jay Conrad Levinson*

"I know that the information one gets after reading *Navigate 2.0* will empower anyone to go out and connect with customers in a meaningful way, and sell to them the way they like to buy."

—**Tony Jeary,** *author of* **Strategic Acceleration**

"As the all-time record holder in sales for the Southwestern Company, as the number-one first-year dealer prior to that, and as an effective manager and recruiter, Dustin Hillis is a master of execution and a true student of the game. *Navigate* defines both basic and advanced techniques developed by Southwestern Consulting™ and used by Hillis in the trenches. It is a must-read for sales professionals interested in going to the next level."

—**Henry Bedford,** *CEO and chairman of the board of* **Southwestern Family of Companies**

DEDICATION

This book is dedicated to the wandering souls out there who are trying to fill the empty, God-shaped hole in their hearts with success, accomplishments, or other trivial things. *Navigate 2.0* is not just a book about being more successful in your career and making more money. It's also about being a better human and treating other people the way they want to be treated.

God calls us to love our neighbors as we love ourselves. Hopefully, after reading *Navigate 2.0*, you will be able to communicate better and love your neighbors a little bit better than you did before.

CONTENTS

Introduction 1

Chapter 1   Navigate the Sales Cycle 9

Chapter 2   Identify Your Selling Style 23

Chapter 3   Understand the Four Buying Styles 35

Chapter 4   The Basic Ropes of Navigate 47

Chapter 5   Navigate the Pre-approach 61

Chapter 6   Navigate the Approach 91

Chapter 7   Navigate the Introduction 111

Chapter 8   Navigate the Presentation 127

Chapter 9   Navigate the Close 145

Chapter 10   Navigate the Tough Ones 165

Chapter 11   Navigate from the Heart 183

Acknowledgments 189

About the Authors 191

Take Your Business to the Next Level 195

INTRODUCTION

TROUBLED WATERS

Have you ever felt slammed by the ups and downs of sales? You're trying your best, but these people are unreasonable. They bark at you to get to the point when you're only trying to be nice to them. Or they chat on and on when you've got six other appointments to get to, and you just need them to sign on the dotted line already.

When you try to show them the big picture of how your product will transform their lives, it seems like all they want to do is grill you on endless, mind-numbing details. And then there are the times when you spend an hour with people who nod encouragingly at everything you say, only to tell you they're not interested when you go to make the sale.

Even when you're at the top of your game—presenting every fact, answering every objection, demonstrating the need—you still just can't seem to close the deal sometimes. Some days, your job feels like an endless cycle of annoyance and frustration. It doesn't help that the colleague next to you connects with all kinds of different people easily and is making money left and right.

You love the high that comes with closing a deal, but the lows of the sales process take a huge toll on you. You're tired of being stressed out all the time. You're searching for the missing piece in the sales puzzle. You're looking for the key that will transform your career from a roller coaster into a year-round cruise. You're looking for the secret that will take your craft and your success to the next level.

You're searching for a new way to navigate the sales process.

TRUST: SELLING THE WAY PEOPLE LIKE TO BUY

Success in sales revolves around one key thing: trust.

Trust is the honest emotional connection you make with your buyer—a connection that closes the sale. But what makes a buyer trust you enough to invest in what you're selling? Why is it so easy for you to connect with some people and not others?

The answer is actually simple: not everybody likes to buy the way you like to sell.

Think about it. You're trying to build rapport with someone, and the response you get is, "Get to the point; I don't have all day." Or maybe you *are* the kind of salesperson who gets to the point, and all your prospects seem to want to do is banter pleasantries with you or demand every technical fact under the sun about your product.

You can mix and match the combinations any way you like. The bottom line is that, when you treat people the way *you* want to be treated, sooner or later there's going to be a clash.

But when you treat people the way *they* want to be treated, all of that changes.

Suddenly, you're connecting with others on a whole new level. The "unreasonable" people you've been struggling with disappear. Instead, they make sense to you, and you're able to respect and work with them. Your confidence goes through the roof.

Before you know it, you're serving more people and closing more deals than ever before.

The best sales approach out there fosters an authentic relationship with people and creates a genuine bond of trust. Not only do you relate to your prospects on a deep and meaningful level, but you feel secure about the way you communicate. You're emotionally connecting with the people you talk to. Why?

Introduction

Because you're selling the way they like to buy.
Navigate 2.0 is designed to teach you to do exactly that.

DUSTIN AND STEVE: KNOWLEDGEABLE NAVIGATORS

Navigate will help you not just in business, but also in life. We know, because we've experienced its benefits firsthand.

Dustin is the co-founder of Southwestern Consulting™, and Steve is a partner and executive coach with the company. With more than 115 team members and offices in the USA, London, Singapore, Australia, and the Czech Republic, Southwestern Consulting is one of the fastest-growing sales and leadership coaching organizations in the world. Both of us have trained thousands of salespeople, managers, and executives in the same *Navigate* techniques you're about to learn in this book, with phenomenal results.

But *Navigate* wasn't built overnight. This system has been the product of decades of study, passion, and experience—for both of us.

How Dustin Became a Navigator

Thank goodness I turned out okay for a rowdy, redneck, dyslexic C student from the hills of north Georgia. I was an insecure troublemaker who always had a way with words and people. I believe that God has always had a plan for me, because on my own I never would have been able to graduate high school and college, become a talented salesperson, start a successful company, write multiple books, and become a loving husband and the father of a beautiful little girl.

My passion for sales has taken me to some pretty neat places. In addition to being a co-founder of Southwestern Consulting, I'm also the cocreator of the Top Producer's Edge coaching program, and I started Southwestern Consulting's USA Consulting Division. I have personally coached top executives from Fortune 500

Introduction

companies including RE/MAX, Wells Fargo, State Farm, Morgan Stanley, and Verizon, among others. I'm also an international speaker and the number-one salesperson out of 150,000 other top-producing sales professionals in the ranks of Southwestern's more than 160-year-old company history.

But the best part is, I didn't find sales. Sales found me.

I was first introduced to the idea of being a salesperson in college. My dad was the one who brought the possibility to my attention. He sat me down after I had suffered a few concussions from playing football and asked me, "Dustin, what are you going to do with your life?"

"I have no idea," I admitted.

Dad nodded. Then he told me, "I've seen kids over at Southwestern Advantage earn $20,000 in one summer selling books door to door."

All I had to say to that was, "Sign me up!"

The intense world-class training at Southwestern turned me into a selling machine. Of the twenty-five hundred other first-year dealers, I finished number one, earning a check for $36,000 in ten weeks during the summer as a sophomore in college. The next year, I recruited a team of eight salespeople and brought home $46,000 for the summer. I was a top producer for the company, and I thought I was pretty suave.

So it dumbfounded me when, at the end of that second summer, an experienced dealer shadowed me for a day and then declared, "Kid, if you ever figure out what you're doing, you will break the company record."

The company record was $84,000 in profits in fourteen weeks. It sounded out of reach, but I'm the type of person who thrives on doing the impossible. *I'm going to make that goal a reality*, I thought to myself.

And I set out to get to work.

It didn't take me long to figure out that learning to communicate with different types of people was key. I'm an extrovert,

Introduction

and all the extroverted prospects I met just loved me. But there are only so many extroverts in a city. When I ran into people who weren't like me, they slammed the door in my face.

I need to learn how to talk to everyone, I realized. *Not just the people who are like me.*

That started me on a mission to learn about different behavior styles. In school, I changed my major from business to psychology. I took all the personality profile tests I could find—DiSC, Myers-Briggs, you name it. But my first big breakthrough came when I attended a training event called "Selling Like a Chameleon" at Southwestern Advantage. That training didn't just identify different behavior styles. It talked about adapting *who you were* to *how you sold* to different types of people.

Yes, I thought. *Now we're talking.*

Armed with my new Chameleon knowledge, I went out that third summer and shattered the company record, bringing in a personal take-home income of more than $100,000 in fourteen weeks as an upcoming senior in college! This was double my production from the previous year. I was excited, but even then, I knew that breaking the record was only the beginning. I was standing on the foundation of something great.

Not long after that record-breaking summer, I took Steve Reiner's Navigating Behavior Styles training—and it was like "Selling Like a Chameleon" on steroids. Steve's course not only talked about adapting to different people; it got into the real nuts and bolts of how to pull it off. We decided to join forces, merging his brilliant framework with my psychology training and the knowledge I'd gained from reading dozens of books and knocking on thousands of doors.

Navigate 2.0 was born. And even though I was one of its creators, the system continued to help me grow as a salesperson and as a person in general. The concepts in these chapters doubled my income. They made a guy who was a great salesperson into an ultra-producer. And they can do the same for you.

Introduction

How Steve Became a Navigator

I've been a producing sales leader for more than twenty-five years. Along the way, beyond becoming a partner at Southwestern Consulting, I also founded SBR Consulting's US operation, earned Southwestern's Coach of the Year and Top Producer awards, and wrote *Selling on Purpose: A Navigator's Field Guide.* I designed the original *Navigate* framework that inspired the system in this book, but that didn't happen out of thin air. Like Dustin, I got my introduction to sales through the school of hard knocks.

I sold books door to door with Southwestern Advantage for eight summers during and after college. And even though I improved every summer, every day felt like a huge battle.

First, I woke up with a *pit* in my stomach, stressed about hitting my goals. Then I *fought* my way through traffic to make my first appointment. After I got there, I *argued* with prospects who wouldn't let me into their homes to do a demonstration. And even when they did let me in, I always had to overcome their objections and *convince* people to buy.

I loved the feeling of helping people with my product. But I struggled with the highs and lows of sales.

As the years went by, it only got worse. Then, finally, after eleven years with Southwestern Advantage, I signed on with a new company to continue my leadership career—and one of my first requirements was to take a personality assessment. When the results came back, they said, "A-Type Personality: Driver."

With my results-oriented, competitive nature, this was no surprise to me. But it left me with a bigger question: *So what and now what?*

What was I supposed to *do* with this information?

The answer struck me one day during a conversation with one of my managers. In a roundabout way, she was apologizing for how she'd talked to me the day before. "I'm sorry if I came across

Introduction

abrasive yesterday," she said. "I'm a Driver, and sometimes I run people over to get the job done. It's just the way I am."

This was the same person who actually trained the team on personality styles. She knew her standard behavior pattern. But she was doing little to *adapt* that pattern to her interactions with others to improve communication. And that was it. The light bulb went off in my head.

I had found the missing piece.

I didn't waste any time before going out to test my big "aha" in the field. I knocked on more than thirty-six thousand doors, conducted twelve thousand demos, and delivered more than three thousand one-on-one leadership consulting calls. I recruited, trained, managed, led, and motivated more than twenty-five hundred salespeople. All the while, I collected knowledge about how certain behavior styles were best able to adapt to other types of people. Eventually, *Navigate* emerged.

The *Navigate* principles you're about to learn transformed me from an above-average producer who was full of excuses to a top-producing sales professional. More than that, they taught me how to stop being stressed all the time so that I could actually enjoy the sales journey.

And I'm not the only one.

Tried and True

Navigate is tried and true.

It has been put to the test by knocking on hundreds of thousands of doors and calling tens of thousands of top sales executives and professionals across the country. Countless sellers and prospects have already benefited from what it has to offer. We have personally tested the ideas, processes, and techniques in these chapters thousands of times.

Our goal with the *Navigate 2.0* system is to help people understand themselves and their prospects better, and we've seen the

Introduction

results firsthand. Salespeople in every industry have used *Navigate* to meet the needs of their clients, earn more sales, and embrace a life of significance in serving others.

You're next.

THE HEART OF *NAVIGATE*

The famous saying goes, "People love to buy, but hate to be sold."

That concept is at the heart of *Navigate*.

This is not a book about how to manipulate someone into buying your product with tricks and gimmicks. It's not a "get rich quick" manual. These chapters are full of proven, time-tested principles that work, but "proven" doesn't mean "easy." The core fundamentals of becoming a *Navigate* top producer are hard work, a positive mental attitude, and a desire to be a student of the game. Only after you've taken those principles to heart can you begin to outperform your colleagues and push your sales success to the next level.

We like to think of the sales cycle as a flowing river that needs to be navigated. That's why we call this process "Navigate." By the time you turn the last page of *Navigate 2.0*, you will have everything you need to modify your natural communication style to fit the buying styles of others. You will be more confident, win more business, and serve more people.

You will know how to sell the way people like to buy. And that will make you a top-producing sales Navigator.

Chapter 1

NAVIGATE THE SALES CYCLE

THE CATCH-22 OF SALES

Selling can be a tremendously exciting experience.
There's no better feeling than winning that big deal you've worked so hard for. It's like competing in a sporting event. You put everything you have into it, and when you score that winning run in the last inning or make that victory jumper with less than a second on the clock, you feel unstoppable. You're on top of the world.

At the same time, selling can be one of the most stressful experiences we go through. You've probably had one of those days when you wake up in the morning with a feeling of dread in your stomach, worried about hitting your goals and anxious over whom you'll encounter on the way.

Sales really can feel like a roller coaster: you're either really high, or really low. Even when you're getting the numbers you want, the process can take such a big emotional toll on you that you start to question how much longer you can keep this up.

Is this sustainable? you wonder. *Is it really worth the pain?*

The Cure: Navigate 2.0

Here's some good news: "Is it really worth it?" is actually a trick question. You don't have to put up with the lows of the sales process to experience its benefits.

You can eliminate the "low" part of the equation altogether by selling the way people like to buy.

When you learn to Navigate by treating people as *they* want to be treated, the stress disappears from the sales process. You're no longer clashing with everyone you meet, trying to arm-wrestle a deal out of them. Instead, you understand what makes them tick—and how to get along with them. You match your frequency to the behavior style of the person you're talking to, and that eliminates the superficial barriers between you, leaving you free to do what you came for: serve people with products and services that are genuinely in their best interests.

Some people claim that the best way to approach sales is to "stick to your strengths." The problem with that approach is that if you sell only to people who are like you, you're missing out on a healthy 75 percent of the market. And there's just no good reason to do that.

When we say "sell the way people like to buy," we aren't talking about throwing your personal strengths overboard. We're talking about a communication style. The goal here isn't to *become* all the different people you talk to on any given day. The goal is to be able to communicate with them clearly. And that's where the *Navigate* system comes into play.

Navigate is more than just a tool. It's a mindset. You don't want to just read and recite the concepts in these chapters. You want to get a *feel* for understanding the different behavior styles, because that's when you'll really start to make deeper connections and build stronger relationships. That's when your chances of making a great impression and creating powerful emotional bonds with people skyrocket.

Navigate is truly an advanced sales book. That doesn't mean it's a shortcut to success. You have to understand the fundamentals of selling before you can put the more nuanced concepts of *Navigate* to work for you. Even if you already have experience in sales, you always benefit from revisiting the basics. Extraordinary

Chapter 1: Navigate the Sales Cycle

salespeople are the best at doing the ordinary things extraordinarily well.

As coach Bear Bryant used to say to some of the best athletes in the world on the first day of practice, "Gentlemen, this is a football."

This chapter will lay the foundation for an extraordinary *Navigate* mindset, review the basic sales cycle, and chart the course for what lies ahead.

THE EXTRAORDINARY MINDSET

The first key to becoming a successful Navigator is developing an extraordinary mindset.

The difference between an extraordinary mindset and an ordinary mindset is the difference between being a peddler salesperson and a professional salesperson who genuinely wants to serve others and has the prospect's best interests at heart—in other words, a Navigator.

An ordinary mindset is self-serving and ego driven. Many salespeople are wired this way. They communicate with others with the goal of serving themselves. Normally, they frame their words to make themselves look good or to protect themselves from appearing incompetent. They treat others the way they themselves want to be treated without realizing that assuming everyone else in the world wants to be treated the same way *you* do is a form of self-centeredness.

A salesperson with an ordinary mindset:

- Focuses on the sale and pressures people to buy
- Talks more than listens and presents solutions without understanding the prospect's true needs
- Oversells, presenting every aspect of the product regardless of needs

- Neglects to answer objections up front and drags out the sales process
- Closes weakly and fears losing the sale
- Lies or exaggerates the truth to get people to buy
- Hesitates to ask for referrals
- Takes shortcuts and tries to get rich quick
- Makes excuses and has a negative attitude
- Treats prospects the same, regardless of buying style

On the other hand, an extraordinary mindset is focused on serving others. When you have an extraordinary mindset, you take the time to ask questions of the people you talk to, and you care about the answers. You use the knowledge you gain to connect with others in a deep and meaningful way. When that happens, people *want* to do business with you, because they see that you're genuinely concerned about their wants and needs. The old adage that "people don't care how much you know until they know how much you care" is true.

A salesperson with an extraordinary mindset:

- Focuses on providing value and taking the pressure off the prospect
- Listens more than talks, asking great questions to uncover the prospect's needs quickly
- Tailors the sales presentation to address the specific needs of the prospect
- Answers objections before they come up and sells real value
- Closes with the sincere goal in mind of helping the prospect get where he or she wants to go faster

Chapter 1: Navigate the Sales Cycle

- Speaks with integrity and focuses on doing *what* is right, regardless of *who* is right
- Asks for referrals from a place of passion for helping more people
- Does what's needed to get the desired results, even when he or she doesn't feel like it
- Has a can-do attitude and focuses on solutions
- Treats people the way they prefer to be treated by Navigating

With an extraordinary mindset, your focus is on serving, and the byproduct is selling. You close far more deals with an extraordinary *Navigate* mindset than you do with an ordinary one.

THE SALES CYCLE

Selling is a process, not an event. We call that process navigating the sales cycle.

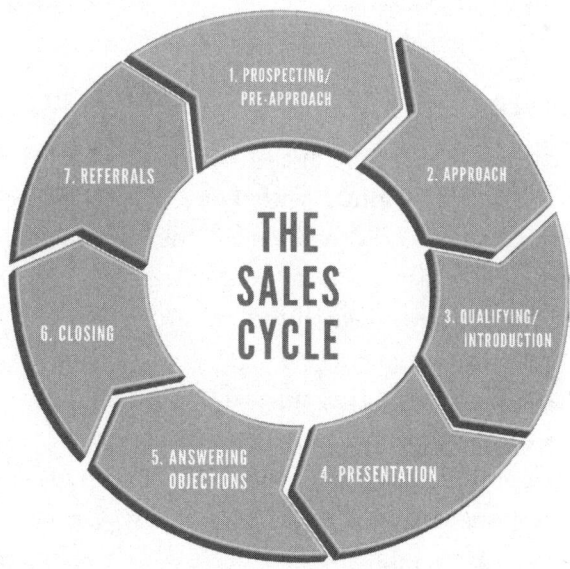

Navigating the sales cycle is the foundation of selling well. It's something that every true student of the game spends a lot of time with, until you understand not just the basics, but also the nuanced ins and outs of the process that make up the fine art of selling. Before you can truly become a top-producing Navigator, you need to be familiar with the cycle of a sale.

The cycle of a sale happens in seven stages: the pre-approach, the approach, the introduction, the presentation, answering objections, the close, and getting referrals.

The Pre-approach

The first stage of the sales cycle is called the pre-approach. This is the part of the cycle where you uncover pertinent information about your leads to help you get in the door with them.

True *Navigate* professionals don't plunge into a sale blindfolded. They do their homework on a client before they engage in a business discussion. By doing some basic research on who they're talking to ahead of time, they're prepared to connect quickly and effectively with their prospects.

The Approach

The approach is the second stage of the sales cycle. This is where you make the initial contact with your prospective client. The approach connects directly to the next stage of the cycle if you're in a one-call, one-close transactional sales business. If not, the intent of the approach is usually to set up an appointment with your prospect, not to make a sale.

The main goal with the approach is to make a good first impression—fast. You have only a few seconds to get people to like and trust you. The prospects you talk to in person will judge you on your nonverbal clues, such as the way you dress, your handshake, your eye contact, and even whether you shine your

Chapter 1: Navigate the Sales Cycle

shoes. And they will make these judgments before you even open your mouth. Even the prospects you speak to over the phone will do the same thing with your verbal clues.

Following a customized script with preempted answers to common objections built into it is usually the best way to handle the approach. We recommend that you create four versions of your script—one for each of the different behavior styles—after you finish the book.

The Introduction

The introduction, or qualifier, is one of the most important parts of the sales cycle, because it is where the sale is actually made! There are five objectives you want to cover in the introduction:

1. *Eliminate distractions.* Always put yourself in control of your environment when you're selling. For example, turn off TVs and radios, position yourself to face the window, and do anything else you need to do to mitigate the potential of your prospect's attention shifting elsewhere during your conversations.

2. *Build rapport and establish common ground.* Typically, the best way to do this is through what Southwestern Consulting senior partner Dave Brown calls "3-Dimensional Names." We don't believe in name dropping, or just saying the names of people you don't really know that well. However, we do believe that telling stories about people whom you and the prospect both really do know well is the quickest way to get people to like and trust you.

3. *Create a buying atmosphere.* Again, people love to buy, but they hate to be sold. Always let people off the hook and let them know that it's okay if they don't buy. For example, you might say, "I'll show you how

this works, and if you like it, that's great. If not, it's no big deal. You won't hurt my feelings if you tell me no. I actually want you to tell me no if this isn't a fit." Without the pressure, your prospect is more likely to buy. Finally, making sure that all the decision makers are present at the meeting right from the start is another key part of creating a buying atmosphere.

4. *Uncover the need.* Without pain, people don't change. Uncovering the need identifies your prospect's pain, needs, and wants. This is where you follow a "needs analysis," or ask a series of questions that uncover your prospects' needs. Doing this allows you to tailor your presentation to their situation.

5. *Answer objections before they come up.* The best way to get rid of objections is to answer them before they come up. In the introduction, the main objections you want to head off at the pass are "I'm not the decision maker" and the procrastination objections ("I want to think about it").

By the end of the introduction, you've positioned yourself perfectly for the next stage of the sales cycle: the presentation.

The Presentation

The presentation is the part of the sales cycle where you actually display the benefits of your product or service.

Many salespeople have the misconception that the presentation should be the longest part of the sales cycle. In reality, the presentation should actually be the shortest part, because you are concisely tailoring your presentation to meet the needs of your specific client. Specifically, you want it to address the pain you discovered during the "uncover the need" phase of your introduction.

Chapter 1: Navigate the Sales Cycle

Your presentation should be entertaining, educational, and inspiring. Don't overdo it by selling past the buying line.

Answering Objections

Handling objections is not a specific step in the sales cycle, but rather a process of continually working alongside your prospects to find solutions of real value. Through the *Navigate* system, you'll learn each of the four buying styles' biggest fears. As you become more knowledgeable about *Navigate*, you'll be able to communicate with each style in a way that alleviates your prospects' natural fears, making them more confident in their purchase and completely preventing the objection from even coming up in the first place.

When objections do come up, the best way to answer them is by isolating the objection; transitioning with "feel, felt, found"; and then providing the answer to the prospect's objection through a third-party testimonial story.

The Close

The close is too often overlooked in the sales cycle. You may identify the problem, establish the need, and present the solution with perfection, but without a proper close, you have no sale.

Closing is about Navigating the pleasure or fear of the buyer. Which one of those comes into play more depends on who you're talking to. We'll give you the specific techniques on how to close for each of the four different behavior styles in chapter 9.

However, one thing is always true about the close: you're helping a prospect make a decision that will serve his or her long-term best interest. Every time.

Getting Referrals

Referrals are the lifeblood of your business because they lead you to new prospects. Working a *Navigate* referral-based clientele is like adding turbo fuel to a Ferrari. You can plant referral seeds early on in the sales cycle by letting prospects know that you appreciate the person who put the two of you together and by asking them to think of others who might benefit from your product or service. Take written notes, and after the close, say something like, "It's been great meeting with you today. I wish I had ten people like you to meet with on a daily basis. If you were me, who would you talk with about this product? My goal is just to let people know what we do. I know you are really involved at the Chamber of Commerce. Who did you sit next to in your last Chamber meeting?"

> **TURBO-CHARGE YOUR REFERRALS**
>
> You can learn to become a referral-generating machine through Southwestern's Top Producer's Edge coaching program, where we teach fifteen different ways to generate leads. To learn more, visit http://FreeCall.TheNavigateBook.com

When you develop a referral-based clientele and apply the *Navigate* principles you're about to learn in the next several chapters, you will increase your business more than you can imagine.

Well-Charted Waters

Top producers don't wing the sales process. They internalize the sales cycle to keep themselves moving toward their goals as quickly and efficiently as possible.

We mentioned in the introduction that the sales cycle is like a river. True Navigators do more than just make it down that river in one piece. They successfully Navigate every part of it. Even with first-time customers, where the landscape is unfamiliar, they feel as though they're in well-charted waters, because the sales cycle is their compass.

Understanding the sales cycle puts you in the deep waters of the "sales channel"—the place where emotional connections are formed, trust is gained, and sales are ultimately made. Now, you just need to meet your passengers.

THE FOUR *NAVIGATE* BEHAVIOR STYLES

The *Navigate* system is built to help you understand the people around you, so that you can connect with your prospects in a deep and meaningful way during the sales cycle. Our years of research have found that people tend to fall into one of four dominant behavior styles: Fighters, Entertainers, Detectives, and Counselors.

Fighters are cut-to-the-chase, bottom-line drivers with little time and less patience. They are motivated by results, and it's important to them to be in control.

Entertainers are social butterflies and enthusiastic extroverts. They love people, possibilities, and rapport—and they care more about emotions than facts.

Detectives are practical analysts. They are always on the hunt for details, and unlike Entertainers, they rank the value of facts over emotions every time.

Counselors are "steady Eddies." Laid-back diplomats, they have the interest of the team at heart. They love security and consistency, and they make decisions by consensus.

These people probably sound familiar. You've met them all before in some shape or form, and a few of them have most likely driven you up the wall in the past. But when you begin to sell to the four behavior styles the way they like to buy, that paradigm of frustration changes fast.

All you have to do is learn to Navigate.

CHART YOUR COURSE

Even before getting to know the four behavior styles, if you truly understand the sales cycle, you probably feel reasonably comfortable at the helm of your ship as a salesperson. But just because your boat isn't sinking doesn't mean you don't have to deal with floods, rapids, and storms. You want to do more than just stay afloat. You want the sales cycle to be smooth sailing.

That's where the advanced techniques of *Navigate 2.0* come in.

The rest of this book will cover the cutting-edge strategies you'll need in order to outperform your peers and become a top-producing Navigator. We've broken the *Navigate* principles down into ten key sections:

> ***Identify Your Selling Style.*** Before you can know others, you need to know yourself. We'll show you how to identify your natural selling style, so that you know where you stand on the *Navigate* playing field. We'll also point out the areas where you have the opportunity to grow as a Navigator.
>
> ***Understand the Four Buying Styles.*** Not everyone likes to buy the way you like to sell. We'll take you through the four different buying behavior styles in depth and give you the rundown on what makes each of them tick.
>
> ***The Basic Ropes of* Navigate.** You know who you are, and you know who you're talking to. The next question is: Now what? We'll teach you the basic ropes of modifying your natural selling style to fit every one of the four buying styles.
>
> ***Navigate the Pre-approach.*** Once you're familiar with the fundamental concept of adapting to the different styles, it's time to put your new knowledge into action—starting

Chapter 1: Navigate the Sales Cycle

with the pre-approach. A big part of the pre-approach is learning to quickly identify which behavior style you're dealing with. We'll walk you through the verbal and nonverbal clues of how to do this for each of the different styles.

Navigate the Approach. After you've identified which behavior style you'll be working with, you still need to know how to say "hello." We'll give you the phrases that connect with each behavior style and show you examples of what does and doesn't work when you're making that first contact.

Navigate the Introduction. Often the most overlooked step in the sales process, the introduction is actually where the sale is made. We'll equip you with an effective process to uncover the need specific to each style, in order to qualify your prospects and create urgency to move forward.

Navigate the Presentation. Even though the presentation should be shorter than most people think it is, it's still a critical part of the sales cycle. There are right and wrong ways to present to each behavior style, and we'll guide you through each of them.

Navigate the Close. Just as with the approach and the presentation, different behavior styles appreciate different types of closes. We'll share the specific dos and don'ts that go into closing all four styles.

Navigate the Tough Ones. Each of us has one style that tends to be the most difficult for us to adapt to. As a true Navigator, you have to be prepared for *every* style. With this in mind, we'll arm you with the right mindset and techniques to embrace even the toughest of styles.

Navigate from the Heart. Anyone can be a salesperson, but only a true Navigator can sell from the heart. The heart of *Navigate* goes well beyond improved sales numbers. In this chapter, we'll show you how.

Transforming from an order-taker into a well-oiled, top-producing sales machine is not light work, and it doesn't happen overnight. But if you're willing to put in the sweat equity, the concepts in these chapters will equip you to connect with people in ways you never imagined were possible.

You'll love Navigating, regardless of who is on the river with you. And the first step in that direction is understanding the person standing at the helm of your ship. In the next chapter, we'll take you through the first *Navigate* principle: identifying your natural selling style.

Chapter 2

IDENTIFY YOUR SELLING STYLE

STEVE'S EPIPHANY: COULD IT BE ME?

Back when I sold books door to door during the summers, I used to get really frustrated with all of the unreasonable people I had to deal with.

For example, I'd knock on a door, and a man with an intense look and tight lips would open it. Before I could get a word in, he'd say, "Not interested."

I'd retaliate with, "How can you tell me you're not interested if you don't even know what I'm doing yet?" *Slam!*

Often, I would spend more than an hour in a kind woman's home, and during the entire demo she'd be smiling quietly and nodding, as if she loved the books. Once, when I was done with my presentation, I asked how the woman wanted to pay for them. She started walking me to the door, thanked me for stopping by, and said she had no interest in buying my product.

I was devastated; I thought she wanted to buy! But instead of shaking her hand and moving on, I said something condescending like, "I'm sorry your kids won't have what they need to improve their grades."

Then there was that woman with the sparkling eyes and spontaneous laugh, who was rollicking with joy during my presentation. At the end of it, she flashed a huge smile and said,

"I just have to check with my husband when he gets back from work. Can you please come back later to collect the check?" That night, I walked half an hour back to her house, all the while calculating my commission on this slam dunk. However, when I knocked on her door at 9:30 p.m. sharp, her husband opened it and said, "We're not interested in your books."

When I looked around for his wife, I made her out in the background, shaking her head and walking away.

And then there were the analytical types who *really* drove me crazy: the ones who asked ten million questions, such as "How long has the company been around?" "How many pages does it have?" and "How many dollars and cents per day does the payment plan work out to?" I tried my best to answer them, but after giving every emotional sales close I had ever learned, I finally walked out of the house empty-handed and furious about how unreasonable they were.

At the time, all I could do was get angry and frustrated about these people who wouldn't buy my obviously wonderful product. One day, I started arguing with a woman who refused to let me into her house to see my books. She ended up calling the police, who promptly came and escorted me away.

As I sat in the back of the police car, I had a realization. Maybe all these "unreasonable" people were not actually the problem.

For the first time, I wondered, "Is it possible that the problem is with me?"

KNOW THYSELF

It's easy to point the finger at others and say, "What's wrong with these people?" But the truth is that the problem isn't the people at all.

The problem is the way you're communicating with them.

Every salesperson has a natural style of selling. We communicate with others the way that we prefer to buy. Therefore, before we can successfully adapt to the different buying styles of the

Chapter 2: Identify Your Selling Style

people around us and sell the way people like to buy, we need to understand how we ourselves work—our strengths and our growth opportunities.

Understanding your natural selling style involves more than just identifying your behavior. It's about helping you uncover *why* you behave the way you do. Why are you motivated some days and not others? Why do you get extremely emotional over some things, while others just bounce right off of you?

You can't adapt your style until you know what needs to change in the first place. When you take the time to understand your selling style, you gain the tools to better adjust to the needs of your buyer. You also gain insight into what to do to achieve your goals.

This chapter walks you through the four types of selling behavior styles, teaches you the key characteristics of each, and guides you through the growth opportunities that will ultimately make you a stronger Navigator.

WHICH BEHAVIOR STYLE ARE YOU?

What is your selling identity?

We introduced the four *Navigate* behavior styles in the last chapter: results-driven Fighters, people-oriented Entertainers, team-focused Counselors, and analytical Detectives. While each of these four styles has fundamentally consistent traits regardless of whether it's applied to buyers, sellers, or anyone else, there are some key things to look for when each style is playing a selling role.

Keep in mind that very few people identify 100 percent with just one style. We are typically a combination of styles, with one dominant and one secondary style in the mix. As we go through each of the four selling styles, ask yourself, "Which of these is most like me? Which is least like me?" You can also think of people you know who fit each of the different types.

Each of the four selling styles has its strengths and growth opportunities. First on the list is one of the more common selling types in the field: Fighters.

Fighter-Sellers

Fighter-sellers are all about the bottom line.

The strengths of the Fighter selling style include great resolve, resiliency, and a willingness to do whatever it takes. If this is your dominant selling style, you are a fast-paced, results-oriented salesperson who needs action. Challenges motivate you. Your motto is ABC: Always Be Closing. You close early, often, and hard.

The flip side of the coin is that Fighters can be so cut-to-the-chase that they barrel through rapport and often lose trust as a result. As a Fighter, you may find yourself constantly wrestling with your pride. You fear losing control of the situation, and under pressure you may lack concern for others and steamroll over people.

With that in mind, here are a few areas where you have the opportunity to grow as a Fighter:

> *Be flexible.* If you look at your track record, you'll probably see that your rigid, cut-to-the-chase style has sometimes lost you sales. How do you overcome this? By learning to be adaptable. Instead of driving straight to the bottom line, allow a little bit of flexibility into your sales cycle. We'll show you how to adapt to different buying styles in the next chapter.
>
> *Serve, don't sell.* As a Fighter, you can be so driven by results that it gives you tunnel vision. This often creates a selling environment where you oversell, the prospect feels pressured by all the dollar signs flashing in your eyes, and you lose deals. The growth opportunity with this is to focus on serving rather than selling. Focus on providing

value by asking more questions, listening, developing trust, and providing the right solutions for your prospects based on their needs. The byproduct of this is more sales, but the sales themselves are not the goal; they're the fruit.

Slow down. When you cut to the chase, you miss the chance to develop rapport and really build that relationship with your prospects. Instead of assuming that you know what the prospect needs, learn to slow down and do a more thorough needs analysis of asking questions and listening.

Cultivate patience. Patience is a big growth area for the Fighter. You always want the prospect to see the value of your product or service before you close the sale. Work with a quiet strength—a relaxed intensity—and take a gentler, humbler approach to people. Learn to be hard to offend and quick to forgive. Your war isn't with your prospects. It's with the six inches between your ears.

At-a-Glance: Fighter-Sellers

- *Strengths:* Resilient, persistent, motivated by challenges
- *Weaknesses:* Impatient, controlling, demanding
- *Motivated by:* Results
- *Fear:* Loss of control
- *Under stress:* Run people over

Enjoy the journey. The more you focus on giving rather than getting as a Fighter, the better results you'll see. Not only do your sales grow, but your peace of mind tends to grow as well. While you can't control your results, you can control the value you provide. It's about learning to enjoy the journey. Instead of telling yourself, "I'll be happy when I achieve my goals," make your new affirmation, "I don't achieve to be happy. I happily achieve."

Entertainer-Sellers

While Fighter-sellers are all about results, Entertainer-sellers are all about people.

If Entertainer is your dominant selling style, then you're very people oriented—and it's one of your strengths. You're naturally full of energy and excitement, and you have the innate ability to transfer those emotions to your prospects, igniting their interest in what you're selling. You're also very expressive, and social recognition is a big motivator for you. Some people might consider you a "smooth talker."

On the other hand, your emotions can run away with you, and you tend to wear them on your sleeve. You may have a tendency to talk too much and overcommit on what you can actually deliver. Under pressure, you become overwhelmed. And because you love social recognition, rejection is a big fear factor for you, so you struggle with the hard knocks of being turned down every day in the world of selling.

Here are some of the major growth opportunities for you as an Entertainer-seller:

> *Schedule more meetings.* As an Entertainer, you may pride yourself on "quality over quantity." That means you schedule fewer meetings with prospects, and the fewer meetings you have, the more important it is to make the sale, which puts a lot of pressure on you. The growth opportunity is to increase your activity. It's all right to rely more on the law of averages than your personal talent. When you do, your attitude shifts from "I need to make this sale" to "It's no big deal if this person doesn't buy from me, because I have fifteen other opportunities lined up that are ready to pop."
>
> *Don't take it personally.* Entertainers tend to base their self-worth on what people think of them. When people are saying nice things about you, you're on top of the roller

Chapter 2: Identify Your Selling Style

coaster, but when they're not appreciative, you hit bottom fast. Your growth area is to learn not to take things personally. You can't control how people respond to you; you can only control the service you give them. Learn to let your confidence come from the knowledge that, at your core, you are doing right by others.

Get organized. If you're an Entertainer, you probably have a tendency to fly by the seat of your pants. You can get into a lot of doors and start the conversation, but you sometimes lack the follow-through to close the sale. And although you're generally very optimistic, when things don't go as expected, you can get bummed out. The growth opportunity here is to get organized. Set clear goals, make a schedule, and execute the plan. Then "hope for the best and be prepared for anything." The more you think things through, the more sales you'll win.

At-a-Glance: Entertainer-Sellers

- *Strengths:* Extroverted, enthusiastic, easily able to transfer emotions
- *Weaknesses:* Talk too much, poor follow-through, minimal attention to detail
- *Motivated by:* Social recognition
- *Fear:* Rejection
- *Under stress:* Become overwhelmed

Tone it down. You definitely have the gift for gab as an Entertainer. And while rapport is usually a good thing, it's probably in your best interest to tone down your time in the spotlight. Remember, you're not the center of attention. Your prospect is. Instead of trying to appear interesting, spend more time cultivating an interest in your prospect by asking more questions and listening to the answers. As John Wayne used to say, "Speak slow, speak low, and don't say much."

Detective-Sellers

In contrast to Entertainers, Detective-sellers couldn't care less about rapport. The things that matter to them more than anything else are the details and facts.

As a Detective-seller, you're one of the most knowledgeable salespeople around. You research every detail of your product and the person you're selling it to, so you know your sales talk better than anyone. You're organized, and you have a logical answer to every objection memorized before you even start the sales process. In a nutshell, you're a perfectionist, and what motivates you most is accuracy.

At the same time, perfection goes both ways. As a perfectionist, your greatest fear is making mistakes, and that tends to slow you down. You can get so caught up in making sure that every last one of your bases is covered that you become paralyzed and never get around to actually selling your product or service at all. Under pressure, you may become critical, of both others and, especially, yourself.

Here are the major growth areas that you have the opportunity to focus on as a Detective-seller:

Focus on progress, not perfection. Because your biggest fear as a Detective-seller is making mistakes, you tend to go to great pains to make sure that you know everything and everyone you're dealing with down to the last detail before you move forward. This can give you "paralysis by analysis": it takes a long time for you to get going, and you don't have enough sales activity. The growth opportunity here is to learn not to let your perfection get in the way of progress. Cultivate a habit of taking action. Just get started, and make course corrections as needed along the way.

Let up. The other downside of perfectionism is that it tends to make you into your own worst critic, pushing you to beat yourself up over the smallest mistakes. Before long, your outlook on things has turned bleak, you're having a hard time bouncing back from adversity, and life in general becomes a struggle. The growth opportunity in this case is to let up on yourself. Learn to be more optimistic by focusing on the big picture of your overall progress instead of the speed-bump mistakes you encounter along the way.

Create a larger vision. If you're a Detective, you might find yourself getting so caught up in the details that you lose sight of your larger goals. Give yourself permission to create a vision for the things you want to achieve in life. Then use it to keep you moving forward with enthusiasm. The amount of your endurance is directly proportionate to the clarity of your vision.

Sell the sizzle. In your practical Detective mind, the sale is made once the prospect understands the logic behind the purchase. That approach works well with other Detectives. However, most people tend to buy based on emotion, not facts and details. If you find yourself selling the steak more than the sizzle, a growth area for you is to learn to connect with people's hearts before their heads by building strong relationships and selling benefits more than features.

At-a-Glance: Detective-Sellers

- *Strengths:* Detail oriented, practical, trustworthy
- *Weaknesses:* Critical, suffer from "analysis paralysis," lose sight of big picture
- *Motivated by:* Accuracy
- *Fear:* Making mistakes
- *Under stress:* Become pessimistic

Counselor-Sellers

Counselor-sellers are focused on maintaining consistency and doing what is in the best interest of the team.

If you fall into the Counselor-seller category, you're probably a fan of guarantees. You're not a lone wolf, and your commitment to supporting the team around you is one of your strengths. Group consensus is your favorite way to make decisions. You genuinely want to help people solve their problems, and you're willing to take the time to get to know your prospects. You're laid back, patient, and a good listener, and asking a lot of questions to build a solid relationship comes naturally to you.

Your natural way of caring for others makes you one of the most approachable of the four selling behavior styles, but it also comes with its share of setbacks. Your determination to deal with people in the least confrontational way possible isn't always in their best interest. You're not a fan of change, and even though you do a fantastic job developing relationships, you can sometimes be guilty of not advancing the sale.

Here are a few areas in which you have the opportunity to grow as a Counselor-seller:

> *Have courageous conversations.* As a Counselor, you may go to great pains not to do anything that could cause friction between you and your clients. Your intentions are good, but what you need to realize is that avoiding controversy is not necessarily helping your prospects. Many people base their decisions on what they feel like doing in the moment. Your growth area as a Counselor-seller is to challenge your clients to make good decisions by having courageous conversations with them about what's really in their long-term best interest. Become a trusted advisor, and learn to be comfortable making people uncomfortable, equipping them to make the hard *right* decision versus the easy *wrong* decision.

Chapter 2: Identify Your Selling Style

Motivate clients to take action by uncovering their pain. Counselors are often called "professional visitors" because they're great at building relationships but not the best at closing sales. You may fear offending your prospects so much that you don't do a good job uncovering their pain. The result is a pipeline filled with people who love you but who have no sense of urgency to move forward. Your growth opportunity here is to learn to motivate your clients to take action by digging deep into their needs and identifying the consequences of not taking action. By learning to challenge your clients this way, you are serving them much better than you would by enabling them to keep procrastinating on their goals.

At-a-Glance: Counselor-Sellers

- *Strengths:* Team player, active listener, consistent, and reliable
- *Weaknesses:* Slow decision makers, bottle up emotions, low energy
- *Motivated by:* Maintaining consistency
- *Fear:* Change
- *Under stress:* Avoid controversy

Sell with enthusiasm. Because Counselors have a laid-back, go-with-the-flow attitude, you can come across as so soft-spoken and mellow to your prospects that they fail to get excited about what you're selling. Remember that selling is a transference of emotion, and learn to inject more enthusiasm into your presentation. When you do, you'll find that your prospects respond with more enthusiasm.

Get out of your comfort zone. You may tend to fear change as a Counselor, and that can make it hard for you to get out of your comfort zone. But without change, it's hard to grow. And as the saying goes, "If you keep doing what you've always done, you'll keep getting what you've always gotten." Remember that fear is like a mirage: the more you face it, the more it goes away. Take action in the direction of your goals, even if it means changing the way things are done. Every time you do, your confidence will increase, and your sales will improve.

CAPTAIN OF THE SHIP

The deeper you dive into the waters of your natural selling style, the more intentional you can be in adapting to your prospect's buying style. You'll know who you get along with naturally, and how to communicate with everyone else to make a meaningful connection anyway. Your sales cycle will be shorter, and you'll win more sales.

You'll have a strong understanding of the captain. And that makes it a lot easier to Navigate the ship.

Once you have a clear grasp of yourself, you're ready to learn the other half of the equation: the behavior styles of your buyers. The next chapter will show you Fighters, Entertainers, Detectives, and Counselors through a buyer's lens and move you one step closer to selling the way people like to buy.

> To learn more about the *Navigate* selling style assessment, visit http://www.TheNavigateBook.com

Chapter 3

UNDERSTAND THE FOUR BUYING STYLES

DUSTIN GETS NAVIGATED

Years ago, I went into a retail store to buy a hat. I was standing in front of the hat display, trying to decide which one I wanted, when a customer service rep walked up to me. "Hey, how's it going?" he asked.

I buy like an Entertainer, so I appreciated the more-than-standard "How may I help you?" line.

"I'm good," I replied.

"Great!" the sales rep said. "What are you getting into this weekend, man? Got any big plans?"

I scratched my head. "Er . . . yeah, actually. I'm heading out to the lake."

"The lake? That's awesome!" he said. "Do you ever go waterskiing? Or kneeboarding? Or tubing, maybe?"

"Sure," I admitted. "I do it all."

"Cool," nodded the rep. "Do you ever hang out on the dock after skiing all day?"

"Yes," I replied.

"Do you drink Corona?"

That was a weird question. "I suppose so?" I responded, confused.

The rep smiled. "Dude, you've gotta check this out," he said, and he gestured for me to follow him over to a shelf, where he picked up what looked to be a pair of regular old sandals.

"Imagine this," he explained. "Later on this weekend, you're out waterskiing all day, having fun on the lake with your friends. You wrap up and get down to your dock, and you're lying out in the sun, relaxing. You reach into the cooler for an ice-cold Corona when, all of a sudden, you realize that you left your bottle opener up at the cabin. Would that frustrate you?"

I felt like I was already there. "Yes!" I blurted.

"Well, what if you had a pair of sandals with a bottle opener in them?" the rep pressed on. "Wouldn't that be pretty cool?"

"Yes!" I exclaimed again, more energized this time.

The rep flipped over the sandals in his hand. There, built into the arch of one sole, was a bottle opener.

I bought those sandals hook, line, and sinker. "Sold! This is amazing!" I told the rep. I didn't even ask how much they were. As I was shelling out money for my new favorite pair of sandals at the register, I realized, *I came into this store to purchase a hat, and now I'm buying these sandals. I've just been Navigated.*

And I loved it!

KNOW YOUR BUYER BETTER

Knowing your natural selling style already puts you in a position to close more deals. But you're still only one half of the buyer-seller partnership. The next tool you need to add to your *Navigate* arsenal is some knowledge about the four buying behavior styles.

For each selling style, there is a corresponding buying style. And just as with selling, each of the four behavior styles looks a little bit different when seen through a buying lens. Understanding the different buying styles is *key* to becoming a top-producing

Chapter 3: Understand the Four Buying Styles

Navigator, because Navigating means adapting to fit your different buyers' needs. You can't sell the way different buying styles like to buy until you understand what makes them tick.

And you can't assume that you already know what makes them tick, either.

For example, just because you're a Fighter-seller doesn't mean you automatically know how to get along with Fighter-buyers. Picture a Fighter-seller who likes to close fast. Now imagine a Fighter-buyer who likes to be in control. You can see the problem already. While the Fighter-seller is laying out her assumptive close, the Fighter-buyer is pushing back because his pride will not allow him to be closed on.

The same kinds of problems crop up between different selling and buying styles as well. Imagine an Entertainer-seller going on and on about the dreamy benefits of her product and how everyone loves working with her. Now put a Detective-buyer on the receiving end of that speech. The Entertainer thinks she's winning over her prospect, but the reality is that she's turning the Detective off, because she's not giving him any facts, and, frankly, he just doesn't trust people who smile that much.

The more you understand the different buying styles, the better you'll be able to put yourself in your customers' shoes and make a real connection with them. This chapter will walk you through the four buying behavior styles and give you real-life case studies of how they express themselves during the sales process.

THE FOUR BUYING BEHAVIOR STYLES

The four buying behavior styles are Fighter-buyers, Entertainer-buyers, Detective-buyers, and Counselor-buyers. And while each buying style has some fundamental qualities in common with its matching selling style, it also has a few characteristics that are tailored to the person on the receiving end of the sale.

Fighter-Buyers

Fighter-buyers need to know the bottom line of what you're selling up front: what are the benefits, what are the risks, and what makes this product or service a good value for them?

Like Fighter-sellers, Fighter-buyers don't have very much patience. Time is more important to them than money, so they're looking to make a decision and move on. They're not afraid of conflict, and they don't really care what other people think of them—especially you, the salesperson.

Fighter-buyers have an aggressive buying style. Like your general Fighter, they enjoy challenges, love winning, and fear losing control. The way those things show up in a buying environment is that the Fighter will insist on controlling the conversation.

Think of the last time you had a selling conversation with someone who knew he was wrong but wouldn't stop arguing with you anyway. The odds are pretty good that you were talking to a Fighter who couldn't admit to the truth because he was so determined to win the conversation.

Each of the four buying styles tends to ask one particular kind of question more than others. The question word that comes up most when you're talking to Fighters is "what." This is literally true in a lot of cases (for example, you'll hear questions such as "What are you selling?" and "What do you want?"), but what you really need to listen for as a Navigator is the spirit behind the questions.

The essence of the question "What?" is that it's all about the

At-a-Glance: Fighter-Buyers

- *Traits:* Controlling, demanding, quick-tempered, abrupt
- *Fear:* Loss of control
- *Under stress:* Take over the conversation
- *Key phrases:* "What do you want?" or "What is the price?"
- *Question:* What?

Chapter 3: Understand the Four Buying Styles

bottom line. You'll hear it disguised sometimes in other forms, such as a curt "Who sent you?" or "Why should I believe this?" But the echo in your ears will sound like someone demanding results. And that's how you know you're dealing with a Fighter.

FIGHTER-BUYER CASE STUDY:

DUSTIN BREAKS THROUGH A BRICK WALL

A few years ago, Dustin created a customized sales script for a consulting client that involved selling medical-grade air-purification equipment. One day, he called on a woman whom a previous client had referred him to.

The first words out of her mouth after she opened the door were, "What are you selling? Actually, you know what? I don't care what you're selling, and I don't have time to listen."

Dustin's natural selling style is an Entertainer, and before he became a Navigator, he would've said something like, "Hi, I'm Dustin. How are you doing today?" But he'd learned to recognize a Fighter when he met one.

He adapted his approach.

"My name is Dustin. The reason I'm here is that I was talking to your friend Nancy, and she told me great things about you. She wanted me to stop by really quick. Did Nancy tell you I was coming?"

"No," barked the Fighter. "What are you doing?"

"The bottom line is that Nancy was telling me that you're interested in your family's health, and the reason I'm here is to talk about your home air quality. It takes five minutes to see if this is something you're interested in. If you like it, great, and if not, just let me know. Nancy thinks you're going to love what we do. Do you have a place where we can sit down?"

The Fighter replied, "You have two minutes."

Not only did she let him in, but she ended up buying Dustin's air-purification equipment after all.

Entertainer-Buyers

Entertainer-buyers love to imagine all the fun they'll have enjoying your product and its benefits. And they love salespeople who will help them create that dream.

Just like Entertainer-sellers, Entertainer-buyers are energetic and outgoing people. When you meet an Entertainer-buyer, you can prepare yourself for an earful, because they love to talk. Before they buy anything from you, they want to build rapport and be your friend. When an Entertainer-buyer and an Entertainer-seller meet, the opening conversation usually goes something like this:

> Entertainer-seller: "How are you doing?"
> Entertainer-buyer: "I'm doing good! How are you doing?"
> Entertainer-seller: "Great! How are you?"

Entertainers are all but professional storytellers. In a buying context, that means you need to be prepared to do a lot of listening if you want to sell to an Entertainer. It also means that they like to hear *stories* about the amazing things they'll be able to do with your product or service. Just remember: the key to selling to an Entertainer is painting a good picture and letting the prospect's imagination do the rest.

Because Entertainers are more people oriented than task or value oriented, the question word that comes up most with them is "who." They want to know "Who gave you my name?" "Who are your other clients?" and "Who else is buying this?" Again, it's the spirit of the

---

At-a-Glance: Entertainer-Buyers

- *Traits:* Extroverted, enthusiastic, make decisions based on emotions
- *Fear:* Rejection
- *Under stress:* Noncommittal
- *Key phrases:* "Who are you?" or "Who are your other clients?"
- *Question:* Who?

Chapter 3: Understand the Four Buying Styles

question that counts, and when the Entertainer asks "Who?" it's all about that person's need to know about other people. "How are you doing?" and "What do most people buy?" are some of the who-type questions you want to listen for as a Navigator.

ENTERTAINER-BUYER CASE STUDY:

ENTERTAINERS OF A FEATHER

One of our consulting clients at Southwestern Consulting is Cellular Sales, Verizon's largest national retailer. Working with Cellular Sales has been a blast, and the team members have been seeing terrific results from our training.

We ended up partnering with them because their director of the National Contact Center and sales manager, Mark, is an Entertainer-Fighter.

Mark had friends at a Fortune 100 company that was also one of our consulting clients. He heard from his contacts there that we were the first outside sales training company that they had ever hired to train their salespeople, and that we'd built a good track record with them over the years that we'd been their consultants. Because of Mark's relationship with our client, Mark was introduced to Southwestern Consulting. We had a lot of fun with Mark in Vegas at our client company's event, and after having a blast together there, we became friends, and Cellular Sales—Verizon's largest distributor—became a client of Southwestern Consulting.

The combination of Mark's trust in his earlier contacts and the relationship building we did in Vegas was largely the reason that Mark requested a consulting proposal from us. And the rest is history. After three months of working with the leadership team at the National Contact Center, we were able to increase the sales team's closing rate by more than 300 percent!

Detective-Buyers

Unlike Entertainers, Detective-buyers have no interest in the imaginative, social elements of what you're selling. Instead, they base their buying decisions on logic and the practical facts and details of why your product or service is the best fit for them.

Like Detective-sellers, Detective-buyers are very logical thinkers. You can almost think of them as human calculators. Everything you say is being calculated, measured, and tested for accuracy in a Detective's mind.

Through a buying lens, a Detective's quest for perfection translates into needing to have all the information before making a buying decision. The biggest fear of Detective-buyers is making a mistake in their research—overlooking some fact that could land them with the wrong product. You can never show a Detective too many details. They love spreadsheets. In fact, one of our business partners is a big-time Detective-buyer, and for Christmas we actually got him a shirt that says, "I love spreadsheets." (He loved it.)

Detectives like to shop around more than any other buying behavior style does. A lot of the time, you'll hear them say things like, "Can you send me some more information? I want to think about this."

The one question that Detectives ask more than any other is "Why?" "Why do I need this?" "Why is it better than the competition?" "Why should I buy it from you today?" The essence of this question is that they are looking for a deep, practical understanding of

---

At-a-Glance: Detective-Buyers

- *Traits:* Detail oriented, analytical, unemotional
- *Fear:* Making mistakes
- *Under stress:* Pessimistic about the product or service
- *Key phrases:* "Why is this better than the other product?" or "Why does it cost so much?"
- *Question:* Why?

Chapter 3: Understand the Four Buying Styles

what you're selling. "How exactly does this work?" and "What are the additional features of this service?" are a couple examples of questions that have the Detective-driven spirit of "why" at their heart.

DETECTIVE-BUYER CASE STUDY:

TOUGH CROWD

Dustin has taught *Navigate* at large sales training conferences for years. When he first started out, he handed out feedback forms for the audience to fill out.

After his first presentation, Dustin collected the feedback forms and started reading through them. About 75 percent of what he read was the best feedback a speaker can receive. "Incredible system!" the reviewers said. "Your speech was fantastic!"

The other 25 percent of the forms, however, sang a different tune. "There wasn't enough content," they said. "Too many stories, not enough facts."

Dustin pulled out the video of his presentation, and as he watched it, he realized the irony of what he'd done. All of his negative feedback was coming from the Detectives in the audience. There were no statistics, percentages, or details backing up all the years of research that had gone into the *Navigate* system. It was all about benefits and amazing results.

I geared my whole presentation to the Entertainers, he thought. *So much for Navigating my speech!*

After that, Dustin changed his presentation to include some data and charts about the *Navigate* buying and selling behavior styles. Many Detectives have been rating him as a top-notch speaker ever since.

Counselor-Buyers

Counselor-buyers make slow, methodical buying decisions, and they rarely do it alone.

Counselors in general are team players. Through a buying lens, that usually translates into being very family oriented, or in the case of a company, looking out for the group as a whole. In the same way that Counselor-sellers hate to offend prospects by pushing their products on them, Counselor-buyers are so naturally wired to care about other people's well-being that they're wary of making a decision without getting everyone's consensus first, for fear that it could hurt the group's feelings. This is true down to the smallest things. For example, this is what it looks like when a Counselor-seller and a Counselor-buyer decide to meet over lunch:

At-a-Glance: Counselor-Buyers

- *Traits:* Cautious, team players, desire consistency
- *Fear:* Change
- *Under stress:* Avoid making a decision
- *Key phrases:* "How does this benefit the company as a whole?" or "How will this compare with what we're currently using?"
- *Question:* How?

Counselor-seller:	"Where do you want to go to eat?"
Counselor-buyer:	"I don't know. Where do you want to go eat?"
Counselor-seller:	"It's up to you. What do you feel like eating?"

Because Counselors tend to fear change and are always looking out for the best interests of the group, they prefer to see the big picture before they buy something. This tones down the risk

Chapter 3: Understand the Four Buying Styles

factor and helps them to make a cautious and wise decision that will benefit all parties involved.

The question you hear most often with Counselors is "How?" "How is this going to benefit the team?" "How will this fit into our current system?" and "How long will it take?" are common questions from Counselors. The spirit behind the "how" is safety and caution. "What are the consequences if this falls through?" and "Whom can we depend on if we need help?" are examples of how-driven Counselor questions.

COUNSELOR-BUYER CASE STUDY:

"BUT I LIKE MY REMOTE CONTROL"

One of our consulting clients is a leading satellite television provider, and the team members were having a hard time selling to Counselors. Not because their product wasn't top notch. Not because they couldn't build relationships.

They couldn't sell to Counselors because almost 100 percent of the people they called already had some kind of television service. And they didn't feel comfortable switching.

"I just really like my remote control," the Counselors would say, and the company's reps had no comeback. It didn't matter how great their service or their price was. The Counselors didn't care. They were too uncomfortable with changing things such as their familiar remote controls.

We put some of the company's distributors through our custom *Navigate* training, including specific pointers on how to talk to Counselors. In the training, we equipped them with Counselor buzzwords and phrases such as "reliability," "customer service," and how their product "brought families together." After that, those who went through the training reported that the team was connecting with and selling to more Counselors than ever before.

BUY IN

With a clear grasp of the four buying behavior styles on your side, you're no longer sailing through uncharted waters in the dark. You know exactly who you're dealing with. And that takes a lot of the guesswork out of selling.

But understanding the people who are on your ship is one thing, and actually connecting with them is a different matter altogether. A true Navigator translates the gap between buyer and seller in concrete ways, so that he or she can meet the prospect's needs and sell the way people like to buy. In the next chapter, we'll walk you through the basic ropes of learning to adapt your selling style to each of the buying behavior styles.

Chapter 4

THE BASIC ROPES OF NAVIGATE

STEVE INVESTIGATES: WHICH STYLE IS MIKE?

Which of the four *Navigate* behavior styles makes the best salesperson?

Several years ago, I was training on the four styles at a company when this question came up. The organization had a solid team of very competitive salespeople led by their VP of sales, Mike. The whole team respected Mike as a great leader and salesperson. As everyone started arguing back and forth over which style was the best, another question emerged.

"Well, which style is Mike?"

I went around to every selling-style group and asked their opinion on this. First, I talked to the Fighters. "Mike's a real cut-to-the-chase type of guy," they told me. "He doesn't beat around the bush; he just tells us what we need to do. He's very motivational, a real hard charger. He's definitely a Fighter."

Now, when I talked to the Entertainers, they had something different to say. "Mike is absolutely an Entertainer!" they exclaimed. They shared how much fun he was, and how he was such a great storyteller. "He's always so positive and enthusiastic," they insisted. "No question, he's an Entertainer."

Of course, when I spoke to the Detectives, they were convinced that Mike was a Detective just like them. "He starts and finishes all his meetings on time," they said, listing the facts. "He supports everything he shares with written documentation. He's organized and he really gets into the details. He's unquestionably a Detective."

And the Counselors were sure that Mike was a Counselor. "He really cares about us," they confided. "He takes the time to get to know what's important to us. And he never forces change on us quickly, always gradually. He's super laid back and very approachable. How could he be anything but a Counselor?"

Mike was so good at connecting with the different behavior styles that, even though he was a Detective by default, nobody could agree on what he was. All of the people he worked with thought he was just like them.

THE PLATINUM RULE

Mike was a natural Navigator. And his ability to adapt to any situation made him not only a great leader, but also a great salesperson. So when we go back to the question "Which of the four *Navigate* styles makes the best salesperson?" we come to this conclusion: your natural style is the less important part of the equation. The real key to selling well is being able to adapt to whomever you are communicating with.

What's important is knowing how to Navigate.

Learning to adapt your selling style to connect on a deep, meaningful level with your prospects is where the true magic of *Navigate* happens. No longer are you banging your head against the wall over people who don't make sense to you. Instead, you're selling the way people like to buy, building relationships, and genuinely serving your clients. The stress that used to haunt you all the time disappears, and a sense of well-being and satisfaction takes its place.

Chapter 4: The Basic Ropes of Navigate

All because you're practicing what is referred to by Dr. Tony Alessandra as the Platinum Rule.

You've already heard of the Golden Rule, which is to "do unto others as you would have others do unto you." In other words, treat people the way you want to be treated. The challenge with the Golden Rule in sales, however, is that the way you want to be treated isn't always the same way that your prospect prefers to be treated.

The Platinum Rule takes the Golden Rule to the next level. It says, "Treat others the way *they* want to be treated." Once you start practicing the Platinum Rule, your prospects' walls begin to come down. Their trust for you increases, and a buying atmosphere is born. But how do you actually practice the Platinum Rule?

How do you start Navigating?

It's not as simple as mirroring your prospect. Mirroring means that you're just duplicating your buyer's style. A true Navigator modifies his or her style to serve the person he or she is talking to, and that involves understanding what drives a buyer's behavior in order to best meet that person's needs.

You can think of learning how to Navigate the four buying behavior styles like you would think of learning how to ski. A good skier navigates the slope based on the conditions. If it's icy, you're going to bend your knees to lower your center of gravity. If you're in powder, you're going to keep your skis parallel and balanced evenly. If you come across moguls, you're going to use short turns with a strong pole plant . . . and if there's a tree in front of you, you'd better turn away from it.

This chapter will guide you through the basic ropes of Navigating each of the four buying behavior styles and give you case studies of what these techniques look like when you put them into practice.

NAVIGATE FIGHTERS

You saw in the last chapter that Fighter-buyers make decisions based on what is in it for them. So how do you handle these abrupt, bottom-line buyers?

You handle them by getting to the point right away, letting them be in control, and building rapport on the back end.

Getting to the point right away is essential. Remember, Fighters have little patience and less time. That means you want to build less rapport with them on the front end. Instead of beating around the bush, give them your value statement quickly, and be clear and specific about how your product is going to affect their bottom line. The idea here is that you're aiming to answer their "what" questions right off the bat.

A key strategy when it comes to Navigating Fighters is to let them be in control. This involves avoiding arguments by embracing objections as opposed to trying to overcome them.

You never want to argue with a Fighter who disagrees with you. This is one example of how adapting is not the same thing as mirroring. If Frank the Fighter is abrasive and you mirror that behavior back to him, you might win the argument, but you'll definitely lose the sale. By forcefully overcoming a Fighter's objections, you're basically telling him that his point is not valid. And that immediately puts him on the defensive.

Instead of arguing with Fighters, learn to embrace their objections by responding with questions. If they disagree with you, say, "No problem. May I ask why?" They may vent at you when you do this—and that's a good thing. Think of Fighters as aerosol cans. They're filled with pressure, and when you tap down on the nozzle, the pressure is released. Once you give your Fighter-buyers the chance to get everything off of their chests, they'll be more open and receptive to you.

Let's say you're selling advertising, and your Fighter-buyer tells you, "I already do advertising with XYZ Company." What you

Chapter 4: The Basic Ropes of Navigate

don't want to do is try to overcome that objection by saying, "Oh, well let me tell you why we're *better* than them." As soon as you do that, you're putting your prospect on the defensive, basically telling him he made a bad decision in choosing to do business with the company he's using.

Instead, you want to embrace the Fighter's objection by saying something like, "That's great. What do you like best about working with that company?" Then, when he says he likes their service, you can respond with, "Because service is important to you, I think you're really going to love how we *complement* what XYZ Company does."

Beyond avoiding arguments, you can also adapt to a Fighter-buyer's need to be in control by giving him choices. The Fighter barks, "I'm too busy to talk with you," and you say, "Exactly. That's why I wanted to call you super quick and schedule a time to meet when you have a few minutes. What works best for you, Thursday or Friday?"

The cardinal rule when Navigating Fighters is to steer clear of power struggles. And once you've successfully adapted to their cut-to-the-chase style, you'll notice that they begin to warm up to you, making more rapport welcome on the back end. A good rapport question for a Fighter is "How did you get to where you are today?" Fighters are very proud of their accomplishments, and you can earn points with them by giving them an opportunity to brag about themselves!

CASE STUDY:

STEVE SNEAKS UP ON A FIGHTER

Steve was making appointments with CEOs to discuss Southwestern Consulting's coaching program one day when he came across a particularly terse Fighter.

"Listen, I have *no* time and I'm *not* interested," snapped the CEO as soon as he picked up the phone.

"I apologize," Steve replied. "I didn't mean to sneak up on you. Do you get salespeople calling on you often?"

"All the time," vented the CEO, "and it takes me away from the work I need to get done."

"Well, I understand where you're coming from, and I apologize again for sneaking up on you," Steve told him, unfazed. "The reason I called is that I've heard some great things about you and how you run a tight ship over there. I was just hoping to connect with you for a few minutes to learn more about your sales goals, to see if we might be a fit. I'm actually going to be in your area next week. Would Thursday work for you, or is Friday better?"

And the CEO replied, "Next week won't work, but I've got some time the following Monday."

Steve scheduled that appointment and hung up the phone. Fighter: Navigated.

NAVIGATE ENTERTAINERS

When it comes to Navigating Entertainers, you want to focus on four things: establishing rapport, selling the dream, offering praise and encouragement, and helping them come to a decision.

You learned in the last chapter that Entertainers make decisions based on emotions. That means that they love to dream, and they want to do business with people they like. Even if Emily the Entertainer has a very specific need for your product, she isn't going to buy from you unless she likes and trusts you.

The first part of building that trust is establishing a lot of good rapport. Because Entertainers love to talk, you'll want to build that rapport around asking *them* questions. Give them the opportunity to do most of the talking, and then listen to what they say. One of the best ways to get Entertainers to like you is to give them your attention.

Chapter 4: The Basic Ropes of Navigate

With Entertainers, you need to sell the dream, not the details. Don't bog them down with too many charts and facts, or they'll lose interest. Instead, sell the big picture with plenty of sizzle. Match their energy level by being enthusiastic and positive. Keep things fun by telling stories and sharing some testimonials to get to the heart of their "who" questions. Ask their opinion and dream with them about what they'll be able to do with their new toy. Help them experience your product or service.

Entertainers get their energy and confidence from words of affirmation. As they're telling you stories and dreaming about your product or service, give them genuine, sincere praise and encouragement. When you do, you'll gain Entertainer-friends for life.

The pitfall with Entertainers is that they can get so caught up in their dreams and stories that they have a hard time staying focused on what you're selling. This can be a problem if they're not the only decision maker. Your challenge as a Navigator is to help them make a decision. A great way to do this is to set up an appointment with the other people involved. If you send the Entertainer to meet with the other decision maker without you, there's a good chance she'll leave out a lot of the details—and an equally good chance that you'll lose the sale.

CASE STUDY:

STEVE CONNECTS WITH AN ENTERTAINER

Steve met with an executive VP of a national mortgage company for breakfast. He saw right away that the VP, Jim, was an Entertainer. So he approached the conversation with questions and listened more than he talked, taking a genuine interest in Jim's answers.

"Jim, when Pete told me I had to meet with you, he shared

that you are one of the most passionate leaders he's ever met. So I've got to ask you, what gives you the passion to do what you do?" he began. Jim's entire face lit up, and he smiled from ear to ear. He spent the next fifteen minutes sharing where his fire came from with great enthusiasm.

The same thing happened with Steve's next two questions.

After forty-five minutes, Jim looked at his watch and said, "Holy cow, I've enjoyed talking with you so much, I lost track of the time. Share with me how I can help you."

Steve responded with enthusiasm, "Our mission is simple at Southwestern Consulting. We help people achieve their goals in life through our one-on-one sales and leadership coaching program." He told Jim how the program worked, sharing the story of how Southwestern had helped Pete's team and what a blast the team had had in the process.

That was when Jim stopped him and said, "Sold. Here are the names of my three regional managers. I'll let them know you'll be calling to set up the workshops. If you're as engaging with them as you were with me, I know my team will love you."

NAVIGATE DETECTIVES

Navigating Detectives is the polar opposite of Navigating Entertainers. When you sell to a Detective, you want to trade rapport for details, keep an even keel on your enthusiasm, find out what the prospect's decision criteria are, and set a timeline for the decision itself.

Because Detectives make decisions based on logic, the sales process for them is about gathering information, not socializing. When you meet with Dan the Detective, you'll want to establish much less rapport and be prepared to give him far more details. Detective-buyers need to see charts, graphs, and figures to support your claims about your product or service.

In fact, Detective-buyers are motivated so little by emotion

Chapter 4: The Basic Ropes of Navigate

that if you get too excited about your product, they'll actually assume that you must be covering something up. Therefore, tone down your excitement when you're talking to Detectives. Stick to the facts, and share less of your opinion. Get into the details of answering their "why" questions.

Another strategy for Navigating Detectives is to find out what criteria they'll be basing their decision on. More than any other style, they'll spell this out for you to the letter. Detectives like to do their due diligence, and you'll often hear them say that they need to "weigh their options." By asking them what their decision-making criteria are, you not only understand how to sell your value better; you also help them make a good decision based on their specific needs.

If left to themselves, Detectives tend to give themselves "paralysis by analysis." Their process of analyzing every last detail can be so painstakingly slow that if you don't help them, they might never make a decision at all. Therefore, in addition to asking about their criteria for making a decision, you'll want to ask them about their timeline for making it. Again, more than other styles, Detectives will tend to stick with the timeline they give you.

CASE STUDY:

DELIVERING DETAILS TO A DETECTIVE

A few years ago, Steve met with the owner of a company that sold oxygen tanks. She was excited about our sales program but said we'd have to present it to her partner, the COO of the company.

"What's he like?" he asked her.

"He's extremely analytical," she told him.

So Steve headed over to this Detective's office. Sure enough, the first thing the COO said to him was, "I just want to tell you up front that I'm not interested in all that touchy-feely crap about how your training will help our salespeople sell with less stress and more passion. The only thing I'm interested in is a guaranteed ROI."

Steve nodded. "Absolutely," he said. "Most of our clients are interested in that exact same thing, and I respect you for it. Here are some testimonials from satisfied clients, and here are some pie charts and bar graphs showing how their sales increased over time."

The Detective glanced at the charts with approval. "I'm going to have to really analyze this information and get back to you," he said.

"Of course," Steve agreed. "Let me just ask you this: on a scale from one to ten, how would you rate your level of interest in partnering with us?"

"Probably a five," said the Detective.

"Great. Why not a three?" Steve asked.

"Well, obviously my partner really likes you, and that means a lot to me," he answered.

"Okay," Steve went on. "And now what would it take to get you up to a ten?"

The Detective didn't miss a beat. "I need to make sure that other companies have seen an increase in sales after your training. I'll want to talk to at least three of the companies you've worked with."

Steve agreed that that made sense and gave him the names and phone numbers of three people he could talk to. Then he added, "What's your timeline for making a decision?"

"I will call you in one week," the Detective promised.

Steve replied, "I'll actually be back in your area next Friday. Is a morning appointment all right, or would the afternoon work better?"

"Friday afternoon will work," said the Detective.

When Steve met with him again the following Friday, the COO was ready to move forward.

Chapter 4: The Basic Ropes of Navigate

NAVIGATE COUNSELORS

Finally, you have your Counselors. When you Navigate this behavior style, you want to focus on building genuine rapport, creating a buying atmosphere by taking the pressure off, checking in on the prospect as you go, and including the team.

As with Entertainers, you want to build a lot of good rapport with Counselors on the front end. However, unlike Navigating Entertainers, with Counselors, it's less about swapping fun stories and more geared toward asking questions about them and their team or family.

Counselors are very laid-back, go-with-the-flow types of people. They're sincere about getting to know you. Showing Carol the Counselor that you're willing to take the time to get to know her in return goes a long way toward establishing a strong relationship with her. When you build rapport with Counselors, speak in a casual, personal tone of voice, and show genuine interest in how they're doing.

Another strategy when it comes to Navigating Counselors is to take it slow. Counselors process things methodically. Because of that, you want to check in with them often while you're presenting your product or service to make sure they really understand its benefits. Here are a few examples of questions you can ask:

- How am I doing so far?
- Does that make sense?
- How does that translate to you?
- What do you like *best* about it?

The saying goes that "a confused prospect never buys." If you take things too fast with Counselors, you'll frustrate them. And that's when they end up saying things like, "That's okay, we're just going to pass this time." Even if you have the best product for them, when you attempt to cut to the chase too quickly for the laid-back Counselors, you'll find them pushing you off. Therefore, remove frustration from the equation when you're Navigating Counselors by taking it low and slow.

The other thing you never want to do to Counselors is pressure them. Remember that Counselors fear change. By pushing them toward anything—especially without the consensus of the group—you are driving them into the heart of their fear. Instead, be supportive of their pace, and help them adjust to the possibility of change gradually. Make sure you answer all of their "how" questions.

And the final key to Navigating Counselors is to bring the team into the equation. Counselors are more interested in serving their teams than they are in serving themselves. When you sell to Counselors, discuss how the team will benefit from your product or service as much as possible. You can even ask them directly: "How do you think your team will benefit?"

With Counselors, slow and steady wins the race, every time.

CASE STUDY:

SLOW AND STEADY WINS THE COUNSELOR

We once worked with a Counselor who completely saw the value in our training program. He even admitted that it was much better than the system his company was currently using. There was just one problem . . .

He'd been using the same training company for years. And just the thought of doing anything different with the sales department made him uncomfortable.

"All right," we said finally after doing everything we could to help him get over his challenge without success. "The last thing we want to do is try to force you into something. But we really like you, and we respect what you're doing here. Let's stay in touch."

Chapter 4: The Basic Ropes of Navigate

And that's what we did. We cultivated a good relationship with him in the hope that, somewhere down the road, we'd be able to work together. Whenever we were in the area, we'd pop in to say hello and see how he was doing. We sent him cards throughout the year, wishing him success. Now and then we'd call him up, just to check in and ask how things were going.

Sure enough, after a year of building a real, solid relationship, he decided to partner with us. And from that point on, he became one of our biggest and most loyal clients.

SAIL ON

When you become a Navigator, no matter what kind of buying behavior style you're dealing with, nothing fazes you.

Fighters bark at you, and you embrace the challenge and make the sale anyway. Entertainers talk your ear off, and you learn to enjoy listening. Detectives demand details, and you deliver. And when Counselors take their time making decisions, you slow your pace and enjoy the journey.

You're selling the way people like to buy. And that makes life easier on everyone.

At this point, you have a feeling for the basic ropes of *Navigate*. You know when you're supposed to use short turns in moguls or slide straight across a patch of ice. But even if your ski instructor does a great job explaining those strategies, you still have a lot of learning to do when you actually get out there and hit the slopes for the first time.

The rest of *Navigate 2.0* will break down the exact way to handle the different behavior styles during each of the major stages of the sales cycle—starting with the pre-approach. And when it comes to Navigating, there's one key benefit that comes out of the pre-approach more than any other: identifying your prospect's buying behavior style.

Chapter 5

NAVIGATE THE PRE-APPROACH

PLAY YOUR CARDS RIGHT

The best poker players in the world are known for their ability to read people.

They know what to look for in the other players seated around the table. The smallest movement clues them in to the hand their opponent is holding. They're masters at flushing out the bluffs and identifying the real deals.

The best salespeople in the world have the same talent.

It sounds a little bit like spy games, and in a sense it is. While poker players read their opponents with the goal of defeating them, however, salespeople read prospects with the goal of *helping* them—sometimes before a single word is spoken.

They're masters of the sales game. And thanks to their keen eye, everyone wins.

PREPARE TO KNOW YOUR BUYER

With a clear grasp of *Navigate*'s core principles in hand, you're ready to start conquering the sales cycle one stage at a time. The first stop on that quest is the pre-approach.

You already know that the pre-approach is the step in the sales cycle where you gather information about your prospects.

The pre-approach has the power to tell you exactly who you're dealing with before you ever meet them. It gives you the edge by sending you the clues you need to identify their buying behavior styles.

You can't Navigate the different buying styles until you're able to recognize them when you see them. And you need to learn to recognize them fast. Remember, you have only a few seconds to make an impression as a salesperson. If it takes you half a minute to put two and two together, your confirmation that you're talking to a Fighter is going to come in the form of a door slamming in your face.

The good news is that, with today's technology, the pre-approach has gotten easier. You can get a pretty clear idea of someone's buying behavior style by his or her use of emoticons in text messages, or the way his or her signature appears in emails. A huge amount of information about people is readily available at your fingertips through online tools and social networking sites such as Google, Facebook, and LinkedIn. You can research companies and individuals by looking on their websites for bios and business articles. But the question that still remains is this:

What exactly do you look for when you get there?

This chapter will teach you the "tells" of each buying behavior style. A lot of these appear in the pre-approach, but you can also take away some great buyer-identification clues from the first few seconds of the approach and introduction as well. For the purposes of this discussion, we'll also be including those in this chapter.

The first thing you want to keep an eye out for is referral-based clues.

REFERRAL CLUES

The best way to become a top-producing Navigator is to work a referral system. You should aim to get an average of five referrals

Chapter 5: Navigate the Pre-approach

from every person you meet with. And once you have the names, you can start investigating their buying behavior styles.

This is as simple as asking a few questions of the person who gave you the names in the first place. For example, you might say something like, "What kind of person is Jane? Is she straight and to the point, or is she a talker? Is she really detail oriented or super laid back?"

> **SUPERCHARGED REFERRALS**
>
> For more information about how to create your supercharged referral system, check out Southwestern Consulting's 7 Steps of Asking for Referrals at http://Referrals.TheNavigateBook.com

Based on the answer, you can identify the style of the person in question. "Oh, don't worry; Jane will tell you what she thinks" means that you're going to be calling on a Fighter. "You're going to *love* Jane! She might talk your ear off, but you'll have such a fun time together" indicates that you're heading for an Entertainer. "Jane will ask you a ton of questions" is a good sign that you're in for a Detective, and "Jane is such a down-to-earth, nice person" means you're probably looking at a Counselor.

Collecting hints about prospects during the referral process can give you a great leg up when it comes to identifying buying behavior styles. But it's not the only tool in your *Navigate* pre-approach arsenal.

NONVERBAL CLUES

Nonverbal clues are another terrific way to figure out which style you're going to be Navigating.

People don't always say what they mean or mean what they say—so it's a good thing we have nonverbal communication to help us get to the bottom of things.

There are hundreds of forms of nonverbal communication.

However, we're going to focus on the five types that you can identify during the pre-approach and in those first few seconds of the approach and introduction: office décor, style of dress, body language, face reading, and handshake.

Office Décor

A prospect's office can tell you a lot about his or her behavior style before you even sit down for the meeting, based on what the person buys and puts on display. Here are a few ways to identify the different styles by their workspaces.

Fighters

A common sight in a Fighter's office is a wall with plenty of awards and trophies on display. You might see a Manager of the Year award or a newspaper article about the Fighter prominently displayed. These are all signs of someone who is motivated by accomplishments—otherwise known as results.

FIGHTER OFFICE

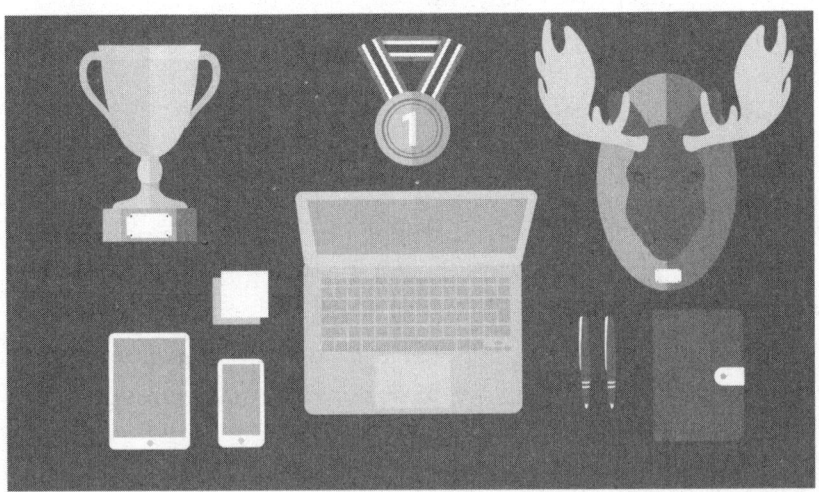

Chapter 5: Navigate the Pre-approach

You could also see things that give you the impression that the prospect is powerful and in control in a Fighter's office, such as expensive furniture or pictures of the person climbing a mountain, skydiving, or hunting. Steve is a Fighter, and he has a fascination with rhinos and buffalo: rhinos for their thick skin and fearlessness, and buffalo for their ability to drive through storms. In his office, he keeps a marble rhino, a wooden buffalo, a book titled *Rhinoceros Success*, and a framed picture with the caption "Be the Buffalo" on it.

Just remember, power equals Fighter, whatever form it takes.

Entertainers

You'll probably see positive affirmations on the office walls of an Entertainer, along the lines of "Act Enthusiastic and Become Enthusiastic!" Entertainers also tend to have some form of a vision board in their space—a collage of everything they want to accomplish in life.

But the real tip-off that you're dealing with an Entertainer is a messy office. Their preferred method of keeping things organized is P.I.P.—"Post-It Planning." Dustin is an Entertainer, and one day a business partner of his walked into his office and tapped him on the shoulder. "Hey, Dustin, you should probably clean your office," the partner said. "We're about to meet with some important clients."

Dustin's response to that was, "I just did."

If you think someone's office is messy, and your prospect doesn't seem to notice, you've probably got an Entertainer on your hands.

Detectives

If messy offices are a sign of Entertainers, tidy offices are the calling cards of Detectives.

In a Detective's office, nothing is out of place. The paper is filed in the filing cabinet. The pencils are in the pencil

DETECTIVE OFFICE

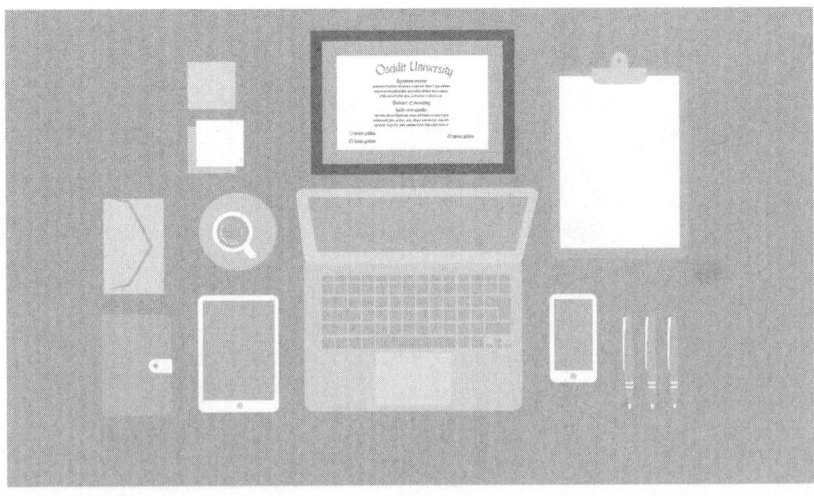

Chapter 5: Navigate the Pre-approach

holders. You'll be hard pressed to find a speck of dust on the desk. There isn't much on the walls, because the walls are cleaner that way.

In fact, Dustin enjoys messing around with Detectives in this area. Once he knows that he's working with one, he'll walk into the Detective's office and set a piece of paper down on the desk cockeyed. Then he'll take a step back and count to see how long it takes for the Detective to straighten up the messy piece of paper. More often than not, the "mess" doesn't last long.

Counselors

The first thing you'll notice when you walk into a Counselor's office is a wall filled with team and family photos. Usually, the display will be pretty prominent. There's generally at least one picture of a group of people doing something in unison with the caption "Teamwork" underneath.

We knew that the CEO of Southwestern—Henry Bedford—was a Counselor the first time we walked into his office, because his son's award-winning elementary school drawing was on the wall, ribbon and all. What really sealed the deal is that Henry's son is now more than thirty years old, and Henry still has that drawing proudly on display.

Style of Dress

A person's style of dress is another useful indicator of his or her buying behavior style.

Everything we put on as we consciously put ourselves together in the morning is a reflection of our subconscious. Not to mention the fact that the clothes, accessories, and shoes we own are things that we've already purchased, so they shine a light onto our buying styles by default.

You don't want to box people into a certain category *just* because they happened to wear a certain type of shirt one day. However, in general, there are a few clothing signs that give you a hint as to which behavior style you're looking at. Keep in mind that, with social media so readily available, you can often spot someone's buying style through that person's style of dress well in advance of your first meeting.

Fighters

Fighters tend to wear solid colors and bold patterns.

For example, a Fighter in business clothes would probably be dressed in a power suit, and that suit would most likely be black, navy blue, or dark gray. You'd probably be able to see your reflection in his or her shoes, which are shined and ready for business. If you ever see a man wearing a solid red tie, that's a good sign that he probably has some Fighter in him.

Chapter 5: Navigate the Pre-approach

Remember, a Fighter's biggest fear is loss of control. The authoritative way this behavior style dresses is tailored to keep the Fighter in the driver's seat.

Entertainers

An Entertainer's wardrobe is full of fun, bright colors and patterns. Things like fancy jewelry, expensive watches, big loopy earrings, and engagement rings big enough to ice skate on are all clear signs that you're dealing with an Entertainer.

For example, a female Entertainer in business attire might wear something like a brightly colored blouse under a coat with big, shiny buttons, and she'd probably pair that with a chunky gold necklace to match the three golden rings on her fingers. A male Entertainer in business clothes would also wear something that pops out, such as large and shiny silver cufflinks, a patterned and monogrammed dress shirt, and a fancy pocket handkerchief.

Keep in mind that an Entertainer's biggest fear is rejection. When they put themselves together, they dress to impress.

Chapter 5: Navigate the Pre-approach

Detectives

Detectives are perfectionists, and their clothes are no exception.

Your average Detectives favor neutral-colored, modest outfits. They usually have their shirts tucked in and their pants pressed. Back in the day, Detectives used to enjoy the organization and convenience of pocket protectors—plastic sheaths that went into the front pocket of a shirt to protect the fabric from the pens you stored there.

As you've learned, a Detective's biggest fear is being wrong. So when he or she gets dressed, you can count on nothing being out of place.

Counselors

Counselors typically dress for comfort. They're so focused on other people that they aren't as concerned with how they look. They tend to stick with earth tones—light browns, tans, warm grays, and greens—because they don't want to bring a lot of attention to themselves.

Counselors' love of consistency is also reflected in their clothing. If you know someone who wears the same type of clothing almost every day, he or she is probably a Counselor.

The Counselor behavior style's fear of change is also accounted for in the way they dress. When you see a person wearing an outfit that is a few decades old, you've probably got a Counselor on your hands.

Chapter 5: Navigate the Pre-approach

Body Language

Like clothing, body language is another instant visual clue to a person's buying behavior style. Here are a few things to look for.

Fighters

Fighters have body language that resembles a drill sergeant. They are usually more intense than your average Joe, and they always seem to be on point, or at attention. When a Fighter walks up to you, he approaches as if he's on a mission, making a beeline for the target and pumping his arms up and down.

A surefire body-language sign of a Fighter is steepled fingers. According to the study of body language, when you position your hands in the steepling manner, it represents the need for control. If someone has a need for control, that someone is probably a Fighter.

Entertainers

If you could take a bouncing ball and turn it into a human, you'd have an Entertainer.

Entertainers bounce and flit around a room, happily waving to people and shaking hands with most everyone they meet along the way. They move as though they're a movie star walking on the red carpet or a politician leaving the stage after a motivational speech: their arms sway with a carefree motion, and they might even wave at you ahead of being within earshot.

In fact, Entertainers love moving so much that they tend to have a hard time sitting still. When the prospect you're looking into speaks with his or her hands and acts fidgety—sometimes to the point of having signs of attention deficit disorder (ADD)—you've almost certainly found an Entertainer.

Detectives

Detectives have body language that resembles a judge in a courtroom.

They tend to sit up straight, and they usually have a pen or

Chapter 5: Navigate the Pre-approach

some other device nearby for taking notes. When they move, Detectives tend to walk from one point to another with calculated steps, carefully observing everyone they come into contact with along the way. They typically keep their body language under control, with little motion in their arms, in order not to reveal anything too deep about themselves.

Detectives are also known for having a skeptical look on their faces. If the body language of the prospect you're looking at gives off an air of discernment, the odds are pretty good that you've got a Detective on your hands.

Counselors

Counselors have body language like a slow-moving bus. Just like a bus, they're comfortable driving along their usual daily route, making frequent stops to make sure that everyone is on board. They walk into a room in a carefree manner with a flow to their walk, and they love the comfort and security of having their hands in their pockets.

Because Counselors are focused on other people, their body language tends to be very open and receptive. You get the feeling just from looking at them that they're ready and willing to listen to what you have to say. Whenever you see someone hanging back in a group, letting everyone else take the spotlight, that person is very likely a Counselor.

Face Reading

In his book *Amazing Face Reading*, Mac Fulfer says, "A face can be read like a map that points the way to a deeper understanding of yourself and of every person you meet." And he's right.

The art of face reading is an ancient practice. It originated more than a thousand years ago in China, where the emperor posted face-readers at the entrance to his palace to tell him what types of people were entering his presence, based on the lines of their faces. The Chinese believe that the lines on your face are a map to your mind.

You can usually identify someone's buying style by the most predominant feature in his or her face. Again, face reading isn't a 100 percent guarantee when it comes to making the identification. However it's usually surprisingly accurate—especially when taken together with other nonverbal clues.

Chapter 5: Navigate the Pre-approach

Fighters

Fighters have two distinct facial features: the freight-train focus line and a hump in the bridge of the nose.

The freight-train focus line is a deep line that forms between the Fighter's eyes. It's the result of a lifetime of intensely focusing on tasks.

The hump in the nose is a sign that when the person in question is backed into a corner, he or she will more likely fight than flee. In high-pressure situations, the gloves come off. But hopefully, when you read your prospect's face right, you'll know better than to argue with a freight-train-lined, hump-nosed Fighter in the first place.

Entertainers

Entertainers have some of the easiest faces to read.

For starters, a round- or oval-shaped head is the first clue that you have an enthusiastic, extroverted Entertainer on your hands. From there, you want to look for round, meaty cheeks. Meaty cheeks are an indicator that someone has spent a lot of time smiling and laughing, and that he or she can maintain high levels of energy for an extended period of time.

Because they laugh and smile so much, Entertainers develop the laugh line. The laugh line appears at the corner of someone's mouth and stretches to the beginning of his or her cheekbone, where it meets the nose. If you see this line, you're looking at an Entertainer, and you'll want to give her a sincere compliment on her wonderful smile.

Chapter 5: Navigate the Pre-approach

Detectives

You can physically see a Detective's analytical mind reflected in his or her facial features.

Detectives often have narrow features. Their heads are usually shaped like a diamond or an upside-down triangle, and many Detectives have a recessed chin. They also tend to have narrower noses, a trait that indicates people who are financially conservative.

Detectives pride themselves on their realism, and you can see this reflected in the lines at the corners of their eyes and mouths, which usually slant downward. Finally, one last sign that you're looking at a Detective is small ears. Small ears indicate that a person is not a risk taker—a characteristic that fits right in with the Detective's biggest fear of being wrong.

Counselors

According to Chinese face reading, Counselors have the element of water in their faces. In other words, their features are very loose and flowing.

One of the most prominent features of Counselors is the nose. A Counselor's nose tends to be large and broad based, meaning that the person is a giver who wants to make sure that everyone is happy.

Low-set ears are another dominant feature in Counselors. Chinese face reading holds that someone with low-set ears is methodical and doesn't make quick, impulsive decisions. Such ears are a perfect match for the Counselor's biggest fear: change.

Chapter 5: Navigate the Pre-approach

The fascinating thing about faces is that they change over time along with the behavior style. For example, we've known people who favored a lone-wolf Fighter selling style in their youth, only to morph into Counselors later in life when they found themselves in more managerial roles. Their faces changed with them, gaining low-set ears and broad-based noses. Your face will adjust to the focus of your mind.

Handshake

The next nonverbal form of communication that can give you insight into the buying behavior style you're dealing with is a person's handshake. Some people say that you can tell whether or not to trust someone by the way he or she shakes your hand. That may or may not be true, but you can definitely tell what kind of buying behavior style you're meeting from a prospect's handshake.

Fighters

A Fighter's handshake is dominant. When a Fighter extends his arm to shake your hand, he moves almost with a jabbing motion, like a sword thrust. A Fighter will typically have a rigid thumb during the handshake itself to indicate authority.

Fighters will also apply more pressure than normal to their handshakes, and they may even turn their hand on top of your hand. These are all ways for the Fighter to assert control, in keeping with his fear of losing it.

Entertainers

When an Entertainer shakes your hand, you can expect a warm, loving greeting. Entertainers are not afraid to extend themselves beyond the normally accepted bubble of personal space. They might be inclined to give you a hug along with the handshake, bump knuckles, or even serve up a high five.

Entertainers will normally come in for a handshake with their palm turned up in a gesture of open, friendly greeting. Picture a big yellow Labrador rolling over by way of saying, "Scratch my belly!" and you've got an Entertainer handshake in a nutshell. With their biggest fear being rejection, they're keen to show you that they just want to be friends.

Detectives

Detectives have the most conscientious handshake of any of the four behavior styles.

In contrast to Entertainers, Detectives tend to be hypersensitive about their personal space. When a Detective reaches out to greet you, he's careful not to overextend, feeling like he might intrude on you. Instead, he reaches out just enough to meet your hand.

A Detective's handshake is usually moderate pressure, one pump, and quick. After he shakes your hand, he may even take a small step back into his familiar comfort zone, where there are fewer chances of making mistakes.

Counselors

A lot of Counselors are pocket people. They don't always offer handshakes right away. Instead, they may keep their hands in their pockets while they analyze the situation, giving you a head nod and turning the other way until they're ready to commit to meeting you. Because Counselors avoid controversy at all costs, they would rather avoid a handshake altogether than lead somebody on before they're ready to move forward.

However, once a Counselor does decide to shake your hand,

Chapter 5: Navigate the Pre-approach

his or her people-loving nature rises to the surface. A Counselor's handshake is soft, warm, caring, and sincere—and once you get it, you know you've also got this prospect's full attention.

VERBAL CLUES

Nonverbal communication will take you a long way when you're identifying the different buying behavior styles. But it's not the only identification tool you have in your *Navigate* armory. Verbal communication can also shed a lot of light on who you're talking to, as soon as you start talking to them.

But learning to recognize verbal communication clues isn't always a straightforward process. People don't always say what they mean or mean what they say. That means you need to learn to listen for not just the words being said, but also the way that those words are spoken.

When it comes to verbal clues, the areas you want to focus on are speaking style, tone of voice, and opening questions.

Speaking Style

While it's true that people don't always mean what they say, the words themselves do usually reflect the speaker's buying style. Let's break down some of the things you can expect to hear from Fighters, Entertainers, Detectives, and Counselors when it comes to overall speaking style.

Fighters

Fighters don't often waste time on pleasantries. When they speak, their sentences tend to be short and choppy, and the words they use can be abrasive.

We mentioned in chapter 3 that each buying style comes with

a dominant question word. Listening for that word when you first start talking to your prospects is a useful way to identify their style. For Fighters, the question word is "what." Again, you're listening for the bottom-line spirit of the word. If your prospect says something like, "What do you want?" or "Just tell me how much it is," you can bet you're talking to a Fighter.

Entertainers

You already know that Entertainers love to talk, and that anyone who talks a lot is a prime suspect for the Entertainer buying style by default. But what do Entertainers talk *about*?

Entertainers often use something cultural to break the ice, such as celebrity gossip or a sporting event. Once the conversation gets going, anything and everything is fair game, and they will talk nonstop with great enthusiasm—sometimes as a defense mechanism, so that they don't have to risk hearing a negative comment about themselves.

To confirm that you're working with an Entertainer, keep your ears open for "who" questions, such as "Who are you?" and "Now, who was it that gave you my name?" "How are you doing?" is a famously common who-spirited question that Entertainers love to ask, whether or not they've met you before.

Detectives

Just as they think analytically and move with precision, Detectives are logical communicators.

As perfectionists, Detectives like to talk about the same thing they think about: details. A Detective's speaking style is thin on emotion but rich in factual content. Because of their sharp discernment, an air of skepticism often finds its way into their voices.

Chapter 5: Navigate the Pre-approach

You also want to listen for the Detective question word, "why," when you're identifying this behavior style. Key phrases can include "Why are you calling?" and "Why is this better than the other product?" as well as less literal comments that still have the fundamental "why" at their heart, such as "Can you explain to me why the price of this is what it is?"

Counselors

Counselors have one of the most introverted speaking styles of the bunch. They tend to stand back and let others do the talking. When they do step in, their speaking style is slow and considerate.

You may remember from chapter 3 that the question word associated with Counselors is "how." The phrases you'll hear from them revolve around concern for others and a desire to maintain consistency in the face of change. "How does this benefit the company as a whole?" "How will this compare with what we're currently using?" and "How is this supposed to work?" are examples of questions you'll hear from Counselors.

Tone of Voice

Another way of identifying a person's buying behavior style using verbal clues is to listen to your prospect's tone of voice. Tone of voice is actually one of the best ways to identify a buying style, whether you're talking to someone in person or listening to a voicemail or online video.

Tone of voice involves two ranges of sound: loud and soft, and fast and slow. Take a look at chart below.

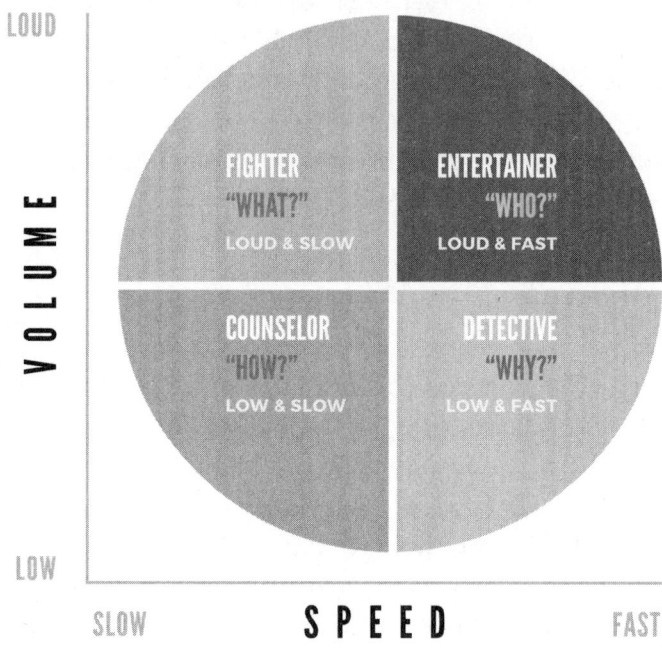

The voice-quadrant diagram was originally created to help teach new speakers how to evoke emotion when delivering a speech. As it happens, the same principles apply to identifying the four different buying styles by the volume and speed of a person's voice.

As you can see in the diagram, Fighters speak loudly and slowly. When you hear them, you immediately get the sense that you're talking to someone with authority. They speak with control, and you can tell pretty easily how they're feeling.

Entertainers also speak loudly, but their pace is faster than a Fighter's. The effect of that combination is enthusiasm reflected in the Entertainer's tone of voice. As with Fighters, it's easy to tell how an Entertainer is feeling.

Detectives use their voices to convey information more than a performance. In person, they speak quickly and in a soft tone

Chapter 5: Navigate the Pre-approach

of voice, giving their words a sense of anticipation, curiosity, and sometimes even skepticism to learn more about the facts. However, be aware that this can change when you're talking to a Detective over the phone. The Detective will still speak softly, but his speed may be slower when analyzing why you are calling. Listen for the cool, analytical aspect of his conversation to distinguish him from a Counselor.

Counselors tend to speak slowly and softly, and the effect that it produces is authenticity. You can usually hear the sincerity in a Counselor's voice, even when she's just saying hello. Although Counselors share a slow pace of speaking with Fighters, their voices are less tonal, because they have no desire to rock the boat or draw attention to themselves.

Identifying buyers through tone of voice is useful for any Navigator, but it's especially critical if your job entails cold-calling. We suggest copying the voice-quadrant chart in this chapter and putting it next to your phone as a reminder of what to look for until you get the hang of this.

It's easy to forget to listen for someone's voice quadrant and dive straight into your sales presentation. But when you train yourself to pick up on your prospects' tone of voice, you can identify your buyer faster and Navigate your way to more sales.

Opening Questions

Another great verbal clue you can use to identify your prospects' buying styles quickly is their response to your opening question.

Our team at Southwestern Consulting is trained to keep a written script with the following opening question on a note card next to the phone:

> Hi. Is this [insert name]? (Pause and wait for a response.) This is [say your first name only, then your first and last name], and if you are trying to put a face with my name it

probably won't work, because we haven't met yet. (Pause and wait for a response.)

We call this script the *Navigate* Opening Question, and it gives us an icebreaker to cut the tension of a sales call. But more importantly, it gives us the opportunity to identify the prospect's buying style.

So how do Fighters, Entertainers, Detectives, and Counselors check out when put through this opening question?

Fighters. Fighters will answer the phone with an authoritative "Hello." Their response to the *Navigate* Opening Question is usually something like, "Okay. What can I do for you?"

Most Fighters are not amused by your engaging opening statement, and you may hear them pause for a second after you say it before they respond with a serious-sounding "Okay." Don't panic when a Fighter responds this way. Your goal at this point is just to identify the buying style. In the next few chapters, we'll show you how to adapt to your discovery once you have the tiger by the tail.

Entertainers. Entertainers answer the phone with an upbeat "Hello!" After you give your *Navigate* Opening Question, an Entertainer will typically ask something like, "Who is this again?" When you repeat your name, the Entertainer will respond with, "Hi, Dustin! Hey, how are you doing today?" Entertainers generally find humor in the opening question, and you might even get a chuckle out of them.

Detectives. When a Detective answers the phone, the "Hello" you hear tends to be spoken quietly, in a quizzical tone. Detectives won't be as irritated by the *Navigate* Opening Question as Fighters, but they won't be amused

Chapter 5: Navigate the Pre-approach

by it, either. "Okay, why are you calling?" they'll respond. Again, don't worry if your Detective doesn't respond to you with open arms. You're just figuring out who you're talking to at this stage.

Counselors. Counselors will answer the phone with a soft, slow "Hello?" When you give your *Navigate* Opening Question, the response will be one of two things. The first is that you may just hear a long beat of silence at the end of the line. The second will be a politely welcoming "How may I help you?" Either way, you'll know that you're talking to a Counselor.

PRE-APPROVED TO CONNECT

There's something magical about knowing the buying behavior style of your prospect before you head in to make a sale. Even if you don't know anything else about the person you're meeting with, identifying his or her buying style gives you the fundamental understanding you need to sell the way people like to buy. That understanding helps the conversation go smoothly. And the smoother the conversation, the more you sell at the end of the day.

Once you know who you're talking to, you're ready to roll up your sleeves and navigate the sales cycle in earnest. In the next chapter, we'll show you how to Navigate all four behavior styles through the next stage of the process: the approach.

Chapter 6

NAVIGATE THE APPROACH

STEVE MARRIES A DETECTIVE

I'll never forget an experience I had with my wife, Kristen, shortly after we were married.

It had been a rough few weeks at work, and I was desperate for a way to let off steam. Finally, on my way home from the office one Friday afternoon, an idea came to me. It was like an epiphany. I could feel my stress melting away already, and I couldn't wait to share my stroke of genius with Kristen.

When I arrived at our house, I threw open the door and announced my well-thought-out plan that I'd just come up with. "Honey," I exclaimed, "let's take off for the weekend. We'll head up to the mountains, get away from email and phones. Let's just drop everything and go!"

Kristen looked at me like I'd lost it.

"We can't do that," she said. "We don't have a reservation, and we can't just show up at some hotel without one. What if they don't have any availability? And what are we going to do with the dog? Besides, it's not in our budget," she finished practically.

Her response sucked the wind right out of my sails. I bit my tongue and just barely managed to avoid saying something I knew I'd regret later.

But I learned my lesson. I was married to a Detective, after all. I learned to adapt my approach to what she considered to be important, and life has been much better ever since.

THE SMART APPROACH

The approach is the first contact you have with your prospect, and you need to make it count. As salespeople, we have only a few seconds to open a potential buyer's mind to us. You might have the best product in the world, but if you can't engage your prospect quickly during the approach, you'll never have the opportunity to share it—let alone sell it.

So how do you make the most of the handful of seconds that you have to make a first impression?

You've already learned how to identify the buying behavior style you're talking to. Now, you need to understand how to adapt your approach itself to win your prospect over quickly. Navigating the approach well is often the difference between being an average sales rep and being a top producer, and it is a crucial part of selling the way people like to buy.

When you adjust your natural selling approach to meet your prospects' buying styles, the door to the rest of the sales cycle opens, giving you the opportunity to connect with people on a deeper level and make more sales.

Each of the *Navigate* buying behavior styles responds best to some very specific techniques during the approach. In this chapter, we'll teach you exactly what those techniques are and give you examples of the right and wrong ways to Navigate each style.

APPROACH FIGHTERS

As salespeople, we're often trained to say, "How are you doing today?" when we approach new prospects. But if you've identified

Chapter 6: Navigate the Approach

that you're talking to a Fighter, that phrase isn't going to do you any favors.

Instead, if you're dealing with a Fighter, you need to tailor your approach to cut to the chase. Bite your tongue on the rapport, and make sure you say the words "The reason I'm calling is" within the first few seconds of conversation. If you're meeting with Frank the Fighter in person, give him a firm handshake and say, "Is it Frank? The reason I came by is . . ."

These words resonate with Fighters, because you're speaking their language. Not only are you straight to the point; you're also answering their innate "what" question right off the bat. When you approach them like this, their mental response is, "Great, you're getting to the bottom line. Let me hear what you've got."

Take a look at these two role plays that demonstrate the right and wrong ways to approach a Fighter.

Navigate Role Play: Approach Fighters

Wrong: Jim approaches Frank the Fighter as an Entertainer.

Jim calls Frank the Fighter.

Jim: *(loud and energetic)* Hey, Frank! How are you on this bright and beautiful sunny day?

Frank: What do you want?

Jim: My name is Jim. Actually, my friends call me "Slim Jim." I'm with Southwestern Consulting, and we are far and away number one in the state in our industry—

Frank: *(interrupts abruptly)* What can I help you with, Jim?

Jim: *(enthusiastically)* Well, I wanted to call to get to know you a little bit, tell you about some of the other incredible people we've been working with, and share with you all about who we are at Southwestern Consulting and what we have going on over here. We focus on quality, speed, and providing outstanding customer service!

Frank: I'm not interested. Take me off your list and do not ever call me back.

Frank hangs up the phone.

Right: Jim adapts his style to a Fighter.

Jim calls Frank the Fighter.

Jim: Hi, Frank?

Frank: Yes.

Jim: *(unemotionally)* My name is Jim, Jim Navigator, and if you're trying to put a face with a name, it probably won't work, because we haven't met yet.

Frank: Okay . . . What do you want?

Jim: *(in a very matter-of-fact tone of voice)* **The reason I'm calling is** that your company came up as one of the top insurance companies in Nashville, and I'm **talking with all of the top-producing companies** in the area such as State Farm and Allstate about their sales teams. I'm with Southwestern Consulting. Have you heard of us yet?

Frank: *(cautiously and only semi-open-minded)* The name kind of rings a bell. But what can I do for you, Jim?

Chapter 6: Navigate the Approach

Jim: Well, **how this concerns you is** that several of the sales managers in the area, such as Bill Anderson and Jane Smith, have brought me in to do a complimentary training with their team to share some ideas related to how to increase the number of referrals they are getting. Do you have **three to five minutes** right now where I can give you a very quick explanation of how it works **to see if it would even be relevant** for you?

Frank: *(direct but curious)* You have three minutes. Make it quick.

Navigate Analysis: In the first scenario, Jim approaches Frank as an Entertainer, beating around the bush with a lot of enthusiasm, energy, and rapport. Fighters become frustrated easily when you approach them in an excitable, longwinded manner, often to the point where they will just hang up on you. Notice the use of superlatives and exaggerated words in the first example. Those are indicators that tip off Fighters easily that they are dealing with someone who is going to waste their time. Additionally, the first example is very self-focused on Jim and his company instead of being focused on what all of this has to do with Frank.

In the second role play, however, Jim gets straight to the point. He uses a more muted tone and eliminates "fluffy" words and language. He also speaks specifically to potential benefits (i.e., increased referrals) as opposed to making loose, broad-sweeping claims (such as "far and away number one . . .").

Another subtle strength of the second role play is that Jim caters to the achiever and ego in most Fighters by indirectly complimenting the success of his team, rather than trying to focus on building himself up. Jim also mentions a specific, concrete timeframe and asks questions that allow Frank to stay in control of the conversation. Most of all, Jim uses key phrases that are music to the ears of a Fighter (the bolded phrases in the dialogue). As soon as he does that, he gets the Fighter's attention. He still has some work to do before he successfully converts Frank into a customer, but because he Navigated the approach well, Frank becomes willing to continue the conversation. If Jim continues on the path that he is on, he will build a strong relationship with Frank in no time.

At-a-Glance: Adapt Your Approach to Fighters

Do:

- Give value statements quickly
- Be clear and specific about the reason you are calling on them
- Challenge them in a positive way
- Answer their "what" questions

Don't:

- Begin with pleasantries or try to build rapport
- Beat around the bush

Key Phrases:

- "The reason I'm calling is . . ."
- "How this concerns you is . . ."

APPROACH ENTERTAINERS

Because Entertainers are people oriented, a great technique to use with them during the approach is to tell a short personal story

Chapter 6: Navigate the Approach

about someone you both know. For example, when you meet Emily the Entertainer, you might say something like, "Hi! How are you doing today? I was just speaking with Jane, and I have heard nothing but great things about you. Jane is awesome, isn't she? The other day I was with her and the funniest thing happened . . . [personal story involving Jane]."

With Entertainers, pleasantries and building rapport are always welcome. The more you encourage a warm, enthusiastic conversation, the better. Here are some examples of the right and wrong ways to approach an Entertainer as a Navigator.

Navigate Role Play: Approach Entertainers

Wrong: Jim approaches Emily the Entertainer as a Detective.

Jim calls Emily the Entertainer.

Jim: Hi, is this Emily?

Emily: *(enthusiastically)* It sure is! How are you doing on this lovely day?

Jim: *(unemotionally)* Hello, Emily. I am doing fine. My name is Jim, and if you are trying to put a face with a name, it won't work, because we haven't met yet.

Emily: *(still excited but a bit confused as to why Jim seems so dull)* No worries, Jim! It's great to meet you! Who are you with?

Jim: *(speaking with a lack of energy)* I work with Southwestern Consulting. We are a part of the Southwestern Family of Companies, which began in 1855. It actually makes us the oldest direct sales company in the United States. We are one of fourteen companies in our corporate umbrella. We have worked with more than seven thousand different sales teams in thirty-five different countries, and we have an A+ rating with the Better Business Bureau.

Emily: *(still trying to be nice but losing interest; her eyes have begun to glaze over with boredom)* Okay, so why are you calling me again?

Jim: Our company specializes in providing tools and systems to sales teams to help them increase their performance. I would like to come into your office to deliver an hour-long informational training to your team.

Emily: *(thinking that the idea of spending an hour with this guy would be dreadfully boring, but not wanting to tell him no for fear of upsetting him)* Gotcha, Jim. Well, thanks for your call, but I actually have to run into a meeting right now. Go ahead and give me a call back later. I gotta run.

Emily hangs up the phone. Jim will spend the next three weeks making two dozen phone calls to Emily as she does everything in her power to avoid having to talk to him and tell him no.

Right: Jim adapts his style to an Entertainer.

Jim calls Emily the Entertainer.

Jim: Hi, is this Emily?

Emily: *(enthusiastically)* It sure is!

Jim: Great! **How are you on this fine day**, Emily?

Chapter 6: Navigate the Approach

Emily: I'm doing good! How are you doing?

Jim: I'm just marvelous! Actually, I was just speaking with **our good friend Kimberly**, and **she had nothing but great things to say about you**. Did Kimberly give you a heads up that I was calling?

Emily: No, she didn't, but I love Kimberly!

Jim: *(without hesitation)* Ha! Yeah, Kimberly is such an **amazing person**. I was visiting with her last week, and she was telling me stories about the golf tournament she played in over the weekend. Did you know she won a hundred dollars for making the longest putt?

Emily: No! Did she really? That's awesome!

Jim: She did! So tell me, **how do you know Kimberly?** Are you guys golf buddies?

Emily launches into the story of how she met Kimberly. Rapport is built, and three minutes go by before Jim even has to explain why he's calling or what company he is with. By that point, Emily feels like they're family and is definitely open to whatever Jim is calling about.

Navigate Analysis: Jim goes down in flames in the first example because he's trying to be all business with an Entertainer. His demeanor is flat, his words are big and logical, and his conversation is loaded with facts and data that seem mind-numbing to an Entertainer. Emily tries to be nice to him and gives him a couple of chances, but she naturally becomes distracted and ultimately starts playing cat and mouse with him. Very ineffective for Jim.

In the second scenario, he does much better by adapting to Emily's buying behavior style. He builds instant rapport and answers her unspoken question—"Who are you and who do you know that I know?"—by using Kimberly as a 3-Dimensional Name that he and Emily have in common. His energy is much higher, and it is easy and natural for Emily to engage with him. He approaches Emily as if he is inviting a friend to a party, rather than asking her to attend a boring business presentation.

We mentioned 3-Dimensional Names in chapter 1. The difference between "dropping names" and using 3-Dimensional Names is enormous. While amateurs just drop names, Navigators describe names, bringing them to life by telling a story about how they know the referral source, or how the referral source knows the prospect. As soon as Jim introduced Kimberly's 3-Dimensional Name, he created an instant connection with his Entertainer prospect. "I like and trust Kimberly," Emily is thinking, "therefore, I like and trust you. I want to keep talking to you."

At-a-Glance:
Adapt Your Approach to Entertainers

Do:

- Begin with pleasantries and build rapport
- Be enthusiastic and energetic
- Use 3-Dimensional Names of people they know
- Answer their "who" questions

Don't:

- Skip building rapport
- Introduce logic and details too quickly
- Be boring

Key Phrases:

- "How are you doing?"

Chapter 6: Navigate the Approach

- "I was just speaking with our good friend Kimberly, and she had nothing but great things to say about you!"
- "How do you know Kimberly?"

APPROACH DETECTIVES

Unlike Entertainers, Detectives *want* you to give them details in the first few seconds of the conversation. When you approach a Detective, you can literally use the words "details" or "facts" and follow them up with some numbers and percentages right away.

Detective-buyers also appreciate it when you tell them up front how long the conversation is going to last. When he hears that you're down to earth and organized and have good content to share, Dan the Detective will decide that you're worth listening to.

Here are two examples of the right and wrong way to Navigate a Detective.

Navigate Role Play: Approach Detectives

Wrong: Jim approaches Dan the Detective as a Fighter.

Jim calls Dan the Detective.

Jim: *(loudly and aggressively)* Hi, Dan?

Dan: *(quietly)* Yes.

Jim: My name is Jim, and I'm with Southwestern Consulting. The reason I'm calling is to set an appointment with you to discuss how we can improve sales in your business. Does tomorrow morning work for you to meet for a quick cup of coffee?

Dan: *(skeptically)* I'm sorry, who is this again?

Jim: Like I said, my name is Jim, and I'm with Southwestern Consulting. The reason I'm calling is to set an appointment with you to discuss how we can improve sales in your business. Does tomorrow morning work for you to meet for a quick cup of coffee?

Dan: *(quickly and with little emotion)* I'm sorry, Jim, but I don't believe I know what this is about. Why are you calling me?

Jim: *(sighs)* Dan, let me just cut to the chase. I'm supposed to talk to all of the sales managers in the area to offer them a chance to have me in to work with their sales team delivering a free workshop. I'd like to block some time to talk with you. Does tomorrow morning work for you to meet for a quick cup of coffee?

Dan: *(confused)* I'm sorry, sir. I'm afraid I'm not following you, so whatever it is that you're selling, I'm not interested. Good-bye.

Dan hangs up the phone.

Right: Jim adapts his style to a Detective.

Jim calls Dan the Detective.

Jim: *(evenly)* Hi, is this Dan?

Dan: Yes.

Jim: Hi, Dan. You and I haven't had a chance to meet yet, but Bill Smith recommended that I give you a quick call. He mentioned that he has a lot of

Chapter 6: Navigate the Approach

respect for you and **how organized and on top of everything** you are in your business.

Dan: Okay.

Jim: Bill thought you might be interested in hearing about the details of a project we've been helping him with. **The project has increased his revenue by 20 percent in the last three months.** Do you have **five minutes** where I could share with you exactly what we are doing and how it works?

Dan: Five minutes?

Jim: Yes, I can guarantee you that if you give me five minutes you will know whether or not this is something that **logically** makes sense for you to explore.

Dan: Okay, go for it. I have a few minutes now.

Navigate Analysis: In the first example, Jim's direct, cut-to-the-chase approach is a turnoff to Detective Dan, who does not trust pushy salespeople and is not interested in being told what to do. Jim's fast pace is also contrary to what is natural for a Detective, who operates a little bit more slowly. While Fighters and Detectives are on the same page when it comes to facts and details, they differ greatly when it comes to pacing. The fact that Jim seems annoyed that he has to slow down is an automatic signal to Dan that this relationship is going nowhere. And because Jim didn't take the time to answer Dan's many questions about *why* he is calling, Dan defaults to saying he's not interested and shuts the conversation down.

But in the second scenario, Jim starts speaking Dan's language. He lets Dan know up front that they've never met, so it's okay to be curious about why Jim is calling. Jim also connects early by showing respect for Dan's organization, following it up with the details of what he wants to discuss and finally offering Dan a timeframe for the conversation. These things earn him Dan's open-mindedness, and the Detective is willing to listen to what else he has to say for at least a few minutes.

Remember, the goal of the approach is not to make the sale. The goal of the approach is to earn a few more minutes with someone to start building a relationship in which you can earn trust and, ultimately, an appointment.

At-a-Glance: Adapt Your Approach to Detectives

Do:

- Be prepared to give details
- Use a controlled tone of voice
- Give them a timeline for the conversation
- Answer their "why" questions

Don't:

- Go too fast or be frustrated if you have to take it slow
- Be overly exuberant
- Be vague about why you're calling

Key Phrases:

- "I can save you X percent in the first X months of your plan."
- "Do you have five minutes to discuss the details?"
- Key words: "logical," "facts," and "details"

Chapter 6: Navigate the Approach

APPROACH COUNSELORS

Because Counselors fear change and are more concerned with pleasing others than themselves, there are four words you can use when you approach Counselors that are music to their ears: team, family, consistency, and growth.

For example, if you're selling real estate, one of the first things you'd talk about in your approach to Carol the Counselor would be how the neighborhood is consistent, growing, and full of stable families. The same concept applies to anything else you're selling. At Southwestern, when we sell large consulting packages to Counselors, we always mention that our training is based on more than 150 years' worth of proven sales strategies, and that it has helped thousands of sales teams consistently grow their revenue by enforcing a set of principles that the whole team can be inspired by.

Compare these two role plays that demonstrate the dos and don'ts of approaching Counselors.

Navigate Role Play: Approach Counselors

Wrong: Jim approaches Carol the Counselor as an Entertainer.

Jim calls Carol the Counselor.

Jim: Hi, Carol! How are you doing today?

Carol: *(long pause, then quietly and slowly)* I'm fine. How can I help you?

Jim: *(enthusiastically)* Great! I'm calling because I wanted to tell you about our incredible sales training program. It can radically transform the way you do business and has been proven to create explosive results! We'll be able to revamp your entire process and take your sales to levels you've never even dreamed about before.

Carol: *(quietly and cautiously)* Oh.

Jim: Yes, you probably know Carol Williams and Mike Smith and a bunch of other people we've worked with. They've all been super excited about how we changed their entire sales process! This is one of the best things you can do for yourself, and I know you'll just be thrilled if you take a bit of time to meet with me. Doesn't that sound like something exciting to explore?

Carol: *(quietly hangs up)*

Jim: Hello? Hello?

Jim calls back and is confused as to why Carol doesn't answer. He thinks that they probably got disconnected and is completely oblivious to how far off he was from relating to her.

Right: Jim adapts his style to a Counselor.

Jim calls Carol the Counselor.

Jim: Hi, is this Carol?

Carol: *(long pause, then quietly)* Yes.

Jim: *(slowing his speech and lowering his volume)* Hello, Carol. It's so nice to meet you. I've been looking forward to building a **relationship** with you. My name is Jim, and I know we haven't met yet, but our good mutual friend Greg passed your name on to me. He had nothing but nice things to say about you. Greg was telling me that you are one

Chapter 6: Navigate the Approach

of his **most trusted friends**, and he suggested that it would be worth my time to contact you because he considers you and me to be a part of his **family**. So he thought I should share how we can **help your team** the same way we helped his. Did Greg give you the heads up that I would be giving you a call?

Carol: No, but he's known for forgetting to do things like that. How may I help you?

Jim: I'm with Southwestern Consulting, and we are a division of the more than 150-year-old coaching and training company Southwestern. We specialize in helping **teams** create positive **consistent growth** in their sales and in **serving their clients**. As I mentioned, we've been working with Greg's **team** for twelve months, and we think of him like **family. Relationships** really matter to us, and so when Greg asked me to call you I was excited to finally **get to know you**. Do you mind if I take a couple minutes to **share** with you what we've been doing to **help his team**?

Carol: Not at all. Please go ahead.

Navigate Analysis: Carol hangs up on Jim in the first scenario because he was talking about revamping an entire process to a Counselor, who avoids change like the plague. Moreover, Jim's focus on enthusiasm, speed, superlative words, and all the people he's been working with acts as a subconscious red flag to a Counselor.

In the second conversation, Jim earns a chance to gain Carol's trust by emphasizing her team and establishing their relationship through a mutually trusted friend. He also slows down considerably and emphasizes some key vernacular that demonstrates he is interested in steady and consistent growth, serving people, and building relationships. Once he makes that connection, Carol becomes much more receptive and willing to hear him out.

At-a-Glance: Adapt Your Approach to Counselors

Do:
- Take it slow
- Mention consistency, growth, and their family or team
- Tone it down and speak in a casual, personal manner
- Answer their "how" questions

Don't:
- Come on too strong
- Focus on what's in it for them
- Scare them with promises of drastic change

Key Phrases:
- "Our program will benefit your team/family by . . ."
- "This X-year plan will promote consistent growth in your team."
- "We love building relationships and serving people."

AND WE'RE OFF

You really don't get a second chance to make a first impression. Learning to Navigate the approach with the four buying behavior

Chapter 6: Navigate the Approach

styles takes discipline, practice, and awareness—especially if you're identifying your buyer at the same time you're meeting him or her for the first time. The more you drill yourself on these techniques, the more natural they'll become, and the more doors will open to you.

Naturally, the next question then is: What do you do once you're in the door?

In the next chapter, we'll walk you through the introduction step of the sales cycle for each of the four *Navigate* buying behavior styles.

NAVIGATE CASE STUDY:

MICHAEL SHERER

Michael Sherer is a top sales manager for AnnieMac Home Mortgage.

I'm the type of person who will do whatever it takes to achieve the goal. Before I found *Navigate*, like most Fighters, I used to react immediately and emotionally during times of stress, baring my claws and teeth in an effort to control the situation to get the desired result.

Then one day, I lost a valuable team member over a bull-headed Fighter-to-Fighter argument. His aggressive response to a comment of mine triggered my own aggressive response, and things escalated to the point that he actually left. In hindsight, I felt completely responsible, because I'd put somebody in a position where he didn't feel secure. The light bulb went on, and I recognized the incongruence between my purpose to serve the team and my controlling actions.

Navigate helped me put the tools in place to overcome my need to be in control all the time. It showed me that the foundation of being able to help others is to communicate with them in a way that will allow them to receive the message well. Now, when I'm faced with another Fighter and I feel my blood pressure rising, I'm able to remind myself, "It's not about me. It's about serving the team." I take a deep breath and really listen to where the other person is coming from, rather than seeing red and charging straight ahead.

Since becoming a Navigator, I've been able to head off conflict and handle situations with more strategy and less emotion. In the past, I used to have trouble connecting with my audience because of the way I was delivering the message. Now, there's an underlying confidence in me. No matter what situation I walk into, I'm fearless in my ability to meaningfully interact with others and to achieve my purpose of positively impacting everyone I talk to.

Chapter 7

NAVIGATE THE INTRODUCTION

DIAGNOSE YOUR PROSPECTS

Imagine walking into a doctor's office for a physical. Right away, the doctor starts bragging about how he graduated at the top of his class at Harvard. He doesn't ask you any questions. Instead of taking your temperature or blood pressure, he simply takes one look at you and says, "You're going to need surgery."

As crazy as that scenario sounds, salespeople do this all the time. They start to prescribe solutions without taking the time to understand their prospects' needs first.

In other words, they don't do a proper introduction.

THE INTRODUCTION: DIAGNOSE YOUR PROSPECTS

The introduction is the most important part of the sales cycle. This is where you eliminate distractions, establish rapport, create a buying atmosphere, uncover the need, and answer objections before they come up. In the same way that doctors assess their patients before treating them, Navigators use the tools in the introduction to ask questions in order to diagnose how best to serve the person they're talking to.

Salespeople commonly believe that the sale is made in the presentation. In actuality, it's made in the introduction, where your prospect's pain is uncovered. Identifying and drawing out the pain naturally creates a sense of urgency to find a remedy—the product or service you're selling.

The introduction is the most commonly skipped part of the sales cycle by average producers, and the most focused-on part of the cycle by top producers. Once you've completed the five steps of the introduction, the sale is already made. If you do it right, you will know whether your prospect is on the hook to buy before you ever go into your presentation. If the introduction reveals that the prospect is not qualified, top producers are able to simply shake that person's hand and say, "Thanks for your time," as opposed to spending hours going through a presentation with somebody who is not a fit.

In this chapter, we'll walk you through a critical part of the introduction and show you how to uncover and grow your prospect's need in order to create motivation to move forward.

CLASP AND CPR

At Southwestern Consulting, we coach clients to uncover the need with an advanced selling strategy called CLASP. CLASP is a consultative sales process using a focused question framework. The acronym stands for

C: Current situation

L: Like

A: Alter

S: Signer

P: Paint the picture

During the introduction, you take your prospects through each stage of CLASP by asking them what their *current situation* is, what they *like* about it, and what they would like to *alter* about it. Then you make sure that they're the only *signers* (decision

Chapter 7: Navigate the Introduction

makers) involved in the purchase. Finally, you *paint the picture* of them getting what they *like* while improving on what they want to *alter* and invite them into the solution with your product or service—also known as the qualifying question.

The "alter" step in CLASP comes with another inbuilt technique that is really the heart of why this strategy works. That technique is called CPR. CPR in sales is about digging up the pain that the prospect feels in his or her current situation, so that you can resolve it. The acronym stands for

C: Cut open the wound

P: Pour salt in the wound

R: Remedy the situation

C: Cut open the wound

When you cut open the wound right, you are helping your prospects understand that their current situation isn't optimal, and that your product or service has the power to change that. Even if they tell you that they don't know what could be better about their current situation, you can prompt them with questions like, "Could it be the customer service?" or "Could it be the price?" Because the truth is that whatever the situation is, it could always be better.

P: Pour salt in the wound

Pain triggers change. Without dissatisfaction in someone's current situation, he or she will not act to do things differently. Pouring salt in the wound helps your prospects understand the gravity of their painful situation. You can do this by asking effect questions. After they say, "Yes, I suppose the customer service could be better," you say, "Tell me more about that. What are the effects of the lack of customer service to your business?"

R: Remedy the situation

Your product or service is the solution to your prospects' pain. After they are done venting about how dissatisfied they are with their current situation, say, "The good news is that is exactly what we do best."

As with every other aspect of sales, CPR is much more effective if you tailor it to fit the buying behavior style of the prospect you're dealing with. Here are some tips for Navigating each of the buying behavior styles through CPR.

CPR for Fighters

With Fighters, you want to be direct and give them a chance to vent during CPR.

When you cut open the wound with Frank the Fighter, you never want to imply that he was wrong to choose what he currently has, because, as we mentioned in chapter 4, that will put him on the defensive. Instead, you want to focus on what could be *better* about his situation. For example, you might ask, "What would help you get where you want to go faster?" or "What's one thing that could be better about what your current provider is doing?"

After Frank answers, you move on to the P of CPR. The great thing about Fighters is that they will actually pour salt into their own wounds. All you have to say is, "Tell me more about that. Why does the service at ACME Cable frustrate you?" Usually, the Fighter will go on a tirade, and you as the Navigator just have to nod and listen.

The Fighter's venting sets you up to remedy the situation with the R of CPR. "I hear you," you can say. "That's exactly why everybody is switching to SouthwesternTV. We have the best customer service on the planet." And you've got your Fighter on board.

Chapter 7: Navigate the Introduction

CPR for Entertainers

When you take Entertainers through CPR, you want to do it in a gentler, friendlier way. Entertainers are all about acceptance. They want to be accepted, and they tend to extend that acceptance to the people around them—including their service providers.

Cutting open the wound with Emily the Entertainer sounds something like this: "Emily, I know you had good reason for going with ACME Cable. But if there was one thing they could do just a little bit better, what would that be?" You edify the decision she made in the first place and give her a very low entry point to find the improvement. You can make it even easier for her by adding something that you heard about her current provider, such as "Could it be the channel selection?"

Once the wound is open, Entertainers will usually open up and start to talk about the problem. As a Navigator, you pour salt in the wound by keeping up the conversation. "Yeah, you know, I wish they offered more channels, too," you might say. "All my friends and I ever talk about is that show *Highlander* and how awesome it is, but I've heard that you can't get it through ACME Cable. What are some of the shows you wish you had that you currently do not?"

After that, the remedy becomes the next natural part of the conversation. "You know, Emily, that's why the friends who referred me to you and millions of other people have switched to SouthwesternTV. We have every channel you could possibly want," you say. From there, Emily is ready to start dreaming about her new service with you.

CPR for Detectives

The best way to Navigate Detectives through CPR is to appeal to their discernment and rational minds.

Detectives take the time to educate themselves on the products and services they have, and you can make a connection with them by acknowledging that during the first step of CPR, when you cut open the wound. For example, you might say to Dan the Detective, "Now Dan, you seem like a pretty sophisticated decision maker, and I'm sure you've found a few things about ACME Cable that it could improve upon. Based on your analysis, what could be better?"

Once Dan tells you that ACME Cable could improve the timeliness of its customer service responses or its inconsistent billing, you pour salt in the wound by empathizing with Dan about the lack of logic behind those problems. For example, you might say something like, "That sounds impractical. I can see how that can be frustrating. Tell me about how that has affected you."

To remedy the situation with a Detective, offer facts and statistics about why your product or service is better, and try to use the phrase "no-brainer." "You know, Dan," you could say, "that's why it's a no-brainer to switch over to SouthwesternTV. Statistically speaking, 37.5 percent of the people who had ACME Cable in the past have switched over, as of this year."

CPR for Counselors

To Navigate a Counselor through CPR, you need to take it slow, focus on other people, and ask for plenty of input along the way.

As with Entertainers, you want to give Counselors a low point of entry when you cut open the wound. But unlike with Entertainers, you want to focus on Carol the Counselor's team or family when you do this.

For example, you could say, "Carol, if there was one area that would help your family improve the quality of their entertainment just a little bit more, what might it be? Could it be your husband being able to record his favorite show, so that he can be on his own schedule instead of the TV's? Maybe your daughter could record *Peppa Pig* and watch it whenever you and your husband

Chapter 7: Navigate the Introduction

need some downtime, instead of on Saturday morning when you want to go on a walk together as a family?"

When Carol agrees that yes, that would be amazing, you pour salt in the wound by asking questions. "That sounds frustrating. Tell me more about that. How would that affect you?" you can ask. "Does it happen often that TV interferes with your family time?"

Finally, the remedy for the pain should include plenty of safety to make Carol feel more comfortable with changing her service. Include the phrase "peace of mind" if you can. "Our customers have the peace of mind that SouthwesternTV is the most trusted brand among families for the very same reasons we've been talking about."

NAVIGATE CLASP AND CPR

What do CLASP and CPR look like when you actually put them into practice? Here are some examples.

Navigate Role Play: CLASP and CPR for Fighters

Frank the Fighter walks into Jim's car dealership, swinging the door wide. He marches directly up to Jim with his arms pumping at his sides.

Frank: I want to look at midsized sedans.

Jim: *(sticks out his hand firmly)* We can do that. I'm Jim. What's your name?

Frank: *(gives Jim's hand an authoritative shake)* Frank. Listen, I'm kind of in a hurry.

Jim: Well, **let's not waste any time**. So, you're looking for a midsized sedan. About what price range

	are you looking for: a basic $25,000 model or something fully loaded, in the $60,000 range?
Frank:	I want the best bang for my buck.
Jim:	*(nods)* Got it. Now, I want to make sure I know how to serve you best, Frank. Is this car just for you, or is there anyone else involved with this decision?
Frank:	It's just for me.
Jim:	*(leading the way out to the car lot)* Great. So tell me, **what are you driving now**?
Frank:	A Stallion.
Jim:	**What do you like about your Stallion?**
Frank:	I love how much horsepower it has. It really is quick off the line.
Jim:	Got it. And what brings you here today? **What's the main thing you're looking for in a new car?**
Frank:	My Stallion is old. I need a car with a little better gas mileage. And I want something that looks good, too.
Jim:	**What kind of gas mileage does your car have now? What does it look like at the moment?**
Frank:	*(venting)* The gas mileage is terrible. What kind of car gets only eighteen miles to the gallon? They advertised it to be more than that when I bought it. And the darn thing takes forever to get from zero to sixty on the freeway. I'm done with that;

Chapter 7: Navigate the Introduction

> I have places to be. Plus it looks awful—old, outdated. It's a dinosaur. I'm embarrassed to park it in the company lot.

Jim: I hear you. Okay Frank, **if we found something that looked good, got great gas mileage, and had a lot of horsepower, would that be something you'd want to jump on today?**

Frank: Yes. Of course.

Jim: I think we have the perfect fit for you.

Navigate Analysis: Jim pegs Frank for a Fighter as soon as he sees him march into the dealership. So Jim gets straight to the bottom line of what Frank is looking for and what Frank's price range is. He begins walking out to the car lot within the first few lines of conversation to show Frank that he isn't going to waste his time, and he asks his CLASP and CPR questions along the way, painting the picture of the new car for Frank when he says, "If we found something that looked good, got great gas mileage, and had a lot of horsepower, would that be something you'd want to jump on today?" Frank appreciates Jim's direct way of communicating, and he's ready to buy a car.

Navigate Role Play: CLASP and CPR for Entertainers

Emily the Entertainer walks into the dealership energetically, wearing a bright orange dress and big hoop earrings. She bounces from car to car in the showroom before ending up at Jim's desk.

Emily: Hello! How are you doing?

Jim: *(with a wide smile, excitedly)* Outstanding! How about yourself?

Emily: *(laughs)* I would be doing much better if I had something fun to drive!

Jim: *(laughs along)* Well, lucky for you, that's what I'm good at helping people find! What's your name?

Emily: Emily.

Jim: Nice to meet you, Emily. I'm Jim. And by the way, **I love your purple scarf**. My wife has a similar one that she got from New York. Where did you get yours?

Emily replies with a fifteen-minute monologue about the backstory of her scarf.

Jim: That's really cool! So Emily, it sounds like you're **excited** about looking for a new car. **What kind of car are you driving now**?

Emily: I'm in a VW bug.

Jim: **Awesome**! What color?

Emily: Lime green!

Jim: Cool. **What do you like best about the VW?** Why did you choose that one to begin with?

Emily: I loved the color, and it's just so cute.

Jim: Definitely. So **why are you looking to get a new car?**

Emily: It's at the end of its rope, and I need something more dependable.

Jim: I'm sorry to hear that it's on its last leg. **How has the lack of reliability affected you?**

Chapter 7: Navigate the Introduction

Emily tells Jim another fifteen-minute story of a time that she was stranded on the side of the road and missed a terrific party with her friends.

Jim: Got it! Well, we certainly don't want you to miss any more parties. I think we've got something that you're going to absolutely love and look good in, but first I want to make sure I'm not stepping on anyone's toes. **If we did take a look at a car that was dependable, fun, and cute enough for you to drive right now, would it be something that you'd want to move forward with today, or would we need anyone else here to take a look at the car with you**?

Emily: *(smiles)* No, we're all good. It's just me.

Jim: Great. Let's go take a look at it!

Navigate Analysis: Jim identifies Emily as an Entertainer from her flashy clothing and accessories before she even says a word, and he knows that she is a full-fledged Entertainer when she comes up to him and is so enthusiastic. Jim builds rapport with Emily quickly over her scarf, creating a bond of like and trust. He also makes sure to adapt to Emily's emotional decision-making style as he walks her through CLASP and CPR.

Navigate Role Play: CLASP and CPR for Detectives

Dan the Detective walks into the dealership with methodical steps and little movement in his arms, dressed in pressed khaki pants and a buttoned-up collared shirt.

Jim: *(approaches Dan and extends his hand)* Hello.

Dan: *(shakes Jim's hand lightly and takes a small step*

	back) Hello. I'm looking for a new BMW 335i hardtop convertible with a sports package and alloy wheels.
Jim:	*(nods)* Great. You strike me as a man who **knows exactly what he wants**. I appreciate it when guys **do their homework and know what they are looking for**. Now, if I'm reading you right, it seems like you'd probably like to know **all of the details and options** that come with our other BMWs so that you can **compare** them with the model you're looking for. Am I right?
Dan:	*(with a small smile)* Yes, exactly.
Jim:	I'm sorry. My name is Jim. I didn't catch yours.
Dan:	I'm Dan.
Jim:	Good to meet you, Dan. **Do you mind if I jot down some of the specifics** you are looking for in your BMW so that I can identify whether we have one in stock or need to ship one from another location?

Dan doesn't mind, and Jim asks him a series of questions about **what kind of car he has now, what he likes about it**, and especially **what he wants in his new car and why that is essential to him**. Dan gives Jim details on the price range he's looking for, along with color choice, miles per gallon, and other specifications. Then, Jim takes Dan out to the lot and lets him test drive a similar model, all the while explaining **all of the special benefits and details** of the car to Dan. Dan likes the model he drove and buys it, along with the warranty package after Jim reads him **every word of the small print**.

Chapter 7: Navigate the Introduction

Navigate Analysis: Jim knows Dan is a Detective because of the way he dresses, shakes hands, and asks detailed questions. He leads Dan through the CLASP and CPR process while keeping the focus of the conversation on facts, details, and logic, and he gives Dan all the comparisons he needs to make sure that the conversation doesn't end with Dan saying, "I want to think about it." Dan appreciates that Jim takes the time to really find out what he is looking for, which earns his trust and leads to the sale.

Navigate Role Play: CLASP and CPR for Counselors

Carol the Counselor walks into the dealership and slowly strolls around the showroom, as if she's just checking things out. She's dressed conservatively. Jim allows her to wander for a little bit before approaching her very casually, as Carol is looking at an Audi.

Jim: Did you know that the Audi is actually the only car that has a **satisfaction guarantee**?

Carol: *(shakes her head)* No, I didn't know. How is that?

Jim: German cars have such a high-quality manufacturing process that Audi is actually that confident in the brand and work.

Carol: Well, that's very interesting.

Jim: *(smiles, shakes his head, and carefully extends his hand)* I'm sorry. My name is Jim.

Carol: *(gives Jim a sincere handshake)* My name is Carol.

Jim: It's nice to meet you, Carol. Did you come in by yourself today, or did you bring the family with you?

Carol: I left everyone at home.

Jim: I see. Are you looking for something in particular?

Carol: Actually, yes. I'm looking for a new minivan.

Jim: *(nods)* And **what are you driving now**?

Carol: A Jeep.

Jim: **What do you like about your Jeep?**

Carol: *(smiles)* It was cheap.

Jim: *(nods again)* **What *don't* you like as much about your Jeep?**

Carol: I'm finding it's just not as reliable or practical as I need it to be.

Jim: Tell me more about that.

Carol: I just had a baby, and it's more important than ever to have a safer, reliable, and dependable vehicle.

Jim: *(smiles)* Congratulations. And I'm happy to say that **I can definitely help you out with something safe, reliable, and dependable. If we found a minivan that was all of those things today, would you want to have anyone else here to take a look at it with you?**

Carol: Yes, I would need my husband here for sure. We never make a decision without discussing it first.

Jim: That's very wise. I'll tell you what. Let's do this **as a professional courtesy to you and your husband.** Let's find out when is the best time

Chapter 7: Navigate the Introduction

to get both of you here, and I feel confident we will find you a minivan that is **safe, reliable, and dependable for the whole family**. Is your husband available to come in now, or would tomorrow be better?

Jim sets up an appointment with Carol for her and her husband to come in at noon the next day.

They meet with him at the appointed time and end up purchasing a new minivan.

Navigate Analysis: Because Jim recognizes Carol as a Counselor, he makes sure to be patient with her from the get-go. He builds rapport with Carol in a casual, low-pressure way, and as he guides her through the CLASP and CPR process, he emphasizes the things that matter most to her: security, dependability, and family. Jim knows that Carol will not make the decision to buy a minivan without her husband, because Counselors arrive at decisions through consensus. He schedules an appointment for Carol and her husband to return to the dealership together, which eventually leads to the sale.

LISTEN AND SERVE

The introduction is what separates the professionals from the peddlers, the trusted advisors from the order takers. Once you've identified your prospect's needs, you're ready to sell value, which simply means sharing solutions that are important to your prospect. This is what we call Navigating the presentation, and we'll walk you through it in the next chapter.

NAVIGATE CASE STUDY:

TRACIE BONDS

Tracie Bonds is a million-dollar earner with Rodan + Fields, with more than twenty thousand people in her personal organization.

My background is real estate, and I used to do my job and everyone else's in order to get transactions through. At Rodan + Fields, however, I discovered that if I wanted to be successful long term, I was going to have to equip my team with what they needed to be successful. As a Fighter, I've always been motivated, outgoing, confident, and not overly concerned when somebody tells me no. As a result, I did well with recruiting. But getting the people I recruited to duplicate me was a different story.

I started getting pressure from my team members early on, who were saying, "You're not training me." Initially my response was, "What the heck do you need training on?" They were trying to tell me they needed training to help them develop their skills and confidence, and I didn't know how to teach them.

After I found *Navigate*, that changed. I learned to communicate one on one with all different kinds of people. It wasn't an easy transition for me. Approaching others the way they want to be approached took a lot of patience. But I resolved to make that change. I learned to lower my voice and ask the questions that would help me understand my team members' needs better. My business was no longer about Tracie Bonds's agenda. It was about really getting to know people. And as it turned out, that selfless way of doing things came hand in hand with incredible results.

Navigate, combined with my Christian faith inspiring me to serve, gave me the tools to coach my team. Once I gave them what they needed, they took it and ran. Their businesses exploded, and I was able to step back and invest more time with my family. My income skyrocketed, surpassing $3 million in earnings. And it continues to go up.

Chapter 8

NAVIGATE THE PRESENTATION

DON'T "SHOW UP AND THROW UP"

When was the last time you were guilty of "showing up and throwing up" for a sales presentation?

You didn't know who you were talking to. You had no idea what your prospect's needs were, and you definitely didn't adapt to the person's buying style. Instead, you threw all of your product's features and benefits at your potential buyer, desperately hoping that something would stick.

How did that work out for you?

If you're like most salespeople, the answer is that it probably could've gone better. You could have been less stressed and had more confidence. And your prospect could have actually bought what you were selling. Bottom line, it wasn't the best experience you've ever had.

Here's the good news: once you learn to Navigate, you never have to "show up and throw up" again.

THE PERFECT PRESENTATION

Navigating your approach well will get you in front of a lot more prospects. But Navigating your presentation is where you really have the chance to sell value to people.

Even if you didn't have the luxury of knowing which behavior style you were selling to before your approach, by the time you get to your presentation, you should definitely be aware that you're speaking to a Fighter, an Entertainer, a Detective, or a Counselor. That means that you don't have to deal with very much guesswork during the presentation.

Instead, you can focus on presenting what matters to your prospect based on two factors: one, the pain you uncovered in the introduction, and two, his or her buying style. The better you can adapt to the behavior style you're speaking to, the stronger groundwork you're laying for the sale.

Average salespeople think that the presentation should be the longest part of the sales cycle, and that they are selling value by presenting all the features and benefits of their product or service. But top-producing Navigators know better.

As a Navigator, you understand that the presentation should actually be the shortest part of the sales cycle. Instead of sharing all the features of what you're selling, you instead present solutions that are of real value based on the needs you discovered in the introduction and what you understand about your prospect's buying style. With these things in mind, you give a brief, tailored, and engaging presentation. Your prospects are served better, and you walk away with more sales. This is a key element in selling the way people like to buy.

If you've done your homework, identified your prospect's buying style ahead of time, and Navigated the approach and introduction well, your presentation should unfold easily and naturally. But you still need to understand the nuts and bolts of bringing it to life. This chapter will give you specific tips for guiding Fighters, Entertainers, Detectives, and Counselors through a strong presentation.

Chapter 8: Navigate the Presentation

PRESENT TO FIGHTERS

You don't want to waste a Fighter's time during the presentation any more than you do during the approach or introduction. Once you've established that you mean business and that you're there to show Frank the Fighter how your service will solve his problem, you need to deliver on that promise in a direct, no-frills way.

Fighters want to know the practical value of what you have to offer, but that doesn't mean they're interested in hearing you report a lot of statistics. To Fighters, the details of why something works are a waste of their time. Instead of dwelling on the specifics, get straight to the bottom line of how your product helps them, and use action words in your explanation.

One phrase you never want to say to a Fighter during a presentation is "What I think you should do is . . ." Remember, Fighters want to be in control, and they hate being told what to do. That means they are about their opinion first, the opinions of trusted colleagues second, and your opinion last. Always give Fighters options when you're presenting to them so that they retain their sense of being in control.

Here is a role play of what the *Navigate* principles of presenting to a Fighter look like in practice.

Navigate Role Play: Present to Fighters

Wrong: Jim presents to Frank the Fighter as a Detective.

Jim is in the process of walking through a second house with Frank, who has his arms crossed and an anxious look on his face.

Jim: Frank, after this house, I have three more to go over with you.

Frank: I don't have a lot of time. I'm going to need you to cut to the chase.

Jim: I understand, Frank. However, I think it's important as you evaluate these homes that you have your arms around all of their unique features. With this home, for example, you can see the roof is brand new and comes with a fifteen-year contractor's warranty. The last owner also installed storm windows, which cut air infiltration into the house by 64.3 percent. The—

Frank: Jim, I've got to cut you off. I've got things to do today. Please hit me with the bottom line.

Jim: Okay, Frank, but before I go over the price, there are just a few more efficiencies I believe you're going to want to know about. The showerheads and toilets, for example, are all low-flow, which will save you 13 percent on your water bill each month. And—

Frank: Okay, you know what? I'm late for a meeting. I've got to run.

Right: Jim adapts his style to a Fighter.

Frank: I don't have a lot of time. I'm going to need you to cut to the chase.

Jim: Perfect. **I remember you saying** that the main thing you want is bang for your buck. Well, **the bottom line is** that, compared to everything else on the market, these first two homes have the **best quality** craftsmanship and the **best price** and are located in the area of town where home values are experiencing **the most appreciation**. The other homes in this area are priced around $650,000, but these are both listed at $575,000.

Chapter 8: Navigate the Presentation

	For the value you're getting, that's a really reasonable investment, isn't it?
Frank:	*(with a firm nod)* Yes, it sounds good.
Jim:	Great. **Which one do you like better?**
Frank:	The first one we looked at.
Jim:	I couldn't agree more. What do you like best about it: the quality of the house or the location?
Frank:	I like them both.

Navigate Analysis: Notice how frustrated Frank becomes in the first scenario when Jim presents to him as a Detective. Frank doesn't want to hear about all the detailed features of the house that Jim thinks are important.

In the second scenario, Jim addresses Frank's unspoken "what" questions, such as "What is this going to do for me?" "What is it going to cost me?" and "What is my return on investment?" He gets right to the point and tells Frank how the house will give him the best bang for his buck. He also gives Frank options to choose from. It's a good idea to allow your Fighter to be in control of the demonstration whenever possible.

At-a-Glance:
Adapt Your Presentation to Fighters

Do:

- Tell them what's in it for them
- Be clear and specific about how your product will affect their bottom line
- Challenge them in a positive way
- Answer their "what" questions

Don't:

- Give your opinion
- Be vague about benefits
- Beat around the bush

Key Phrases:

- "The reason this will help you is . . ."
- "The options here are . . ."
- "The bottom line is . . ."
- "What's in this for you is . . ."
- "Based on what you said you wanted, here is exactly what you asked for."

PRESENT TO ENTERTAINERS

The key to presenting to Entertainers is to keep it fun. The worst thing you can do is bore an Entertainer with details, especially during your presentation. Remember that Entertainers buy on emotion. They want an experience when they're buying something, and it's your job as a Navigator to create that experience.

There are a few different ways that you can spice up your presentation for Entertainers. Technology, such as tablets, can be a way to get Entertainers more involved in the presentation. Changing the environment by getting them outside the office can be a fun way to mix things up. And telling stories, using visuals, and letting the Entertainer actually experience the feel of your product and service are all great tools to help her get excited about the possibility of owning it.

When you present to Entertainers, dream with them and help them paint a picture of their future once they own your product or service. For example, you might ask them something

Chapter 8: Navigate the Presentation

like, "What benefit would you see yourself enjoying most about this product? Is it the _____, _____, or _____?"

Take a look at these examples of the right and wrong ways to present to an Entertainer.

Navigate Role Play: Present to Entertainers

Wrong: Jim presents to Emily the Entertainer as a Counselor.

On their way to see the first house, Emily tells Jim how excited she is to finally have her own place. She shares how cramped it's been having her friends over at her apartment and how she can't wait to have a bigger space.

Jim: Well, Emily, this first house could be a good value for you. It needs some work, but I think your family will enjoy it once the roof and gutter are repaired. It could be a comfortable home with all of the latest efficiencies, and it's in a nice safe location for your family. What do you think?

Emily: *(yawning)* Um . . . I'm not that excited about it.

Jim: Okay, well let's talk about the school system. I know you don't have children yet, but the high school is ranked in the top twenty in the state. They have a new principal, who has made some great changes, and the drama department is supposed to be top notch.

Emily: You know what? I'm meeting some friends for lunch in a bit. Would you mind driving me back to my car?

Right: Jim adapts his style to an Entertainer.

Jim: Emily, based on what I know about you so far, it seems that you're the type of person **who enjoys having a good time**. One of the best features of this location is that it's only two blocks away from the **most vibrant** part of town. Just imagine being able to walk to wherever you want to go to meet up with your friends! Can you picture how cool that would be compared to where you live now?

Emily: You're not kidding. That would be a blast!

Jim: Now wait 'til you see this finished basement. It's got a great space for your parties, with a built-in kitchenette and wet bar. And check out this backyard! Can you see yourself entertaining back here with this in-ground pool and hot tub?

Emily: I'm already thinking about the Fourth of July party we're going to have. Now what do you think about how the house will appreciate?

Jim: What's awesome is that with a little elbow grease, this house is a great fixer-upper investment. Five years down the road, you'll be **really happy** with its appreciation value. Sound good?

Emily: Definitely!

Navigate Analysis: Jim's first presentation falls flat because he focuses on the work involved just to make the house a *comfortable* and *safe* place to live—attributes that are less important to Emily the Entertainer. In the second scenario, he paints a picture of the house's benefits for Emily, who thrives on the vision of an exciting

Chapter 8: Navigate the Presentation

future. Emily is delighted to dream with him about the blast she's going to have living in that area, and what a terrific investment she's going to have on her hands after putting just a little work into the house.

At-a-Glance: Adapt Your Presentation to Entertainers

Do:

- Sell the big picture with lots of sizzle
- Ask their opinion and dream with them
- Keep things fun by using technology, telling stories, and sharing testimonials
- Be enthusiastic and encouraging
- Answer their "who" questions

Don't:

- Bore them with details, facts, and figures
- Use a spreadsheet to explain things
- Read the back of the contract word for word

Key Phrases:

- "Can you see yourself enjoying . . . ?"
- "Just imagine being able to . . ."

PRESENT TO DETECTIVES

When you present to a Detective, you have the opportunity to share all of the facts and details you had to skip with the Fighter and the Entertainer—and then some. Detectives are interested in all the data you can give them. They make decisions based on logic, so the more you can feed their analytical minds with practical, detailed information during your presentation, the more they'll trust and respect you.

Your presentation to Detectives should include plenty of graphs, charts, statistics, price comparisons, and competitive analyses of the competition. A great tool to have on hand when presenting to Detectives is a spreadsheet. Few things make Detectives happier than spreadsheets do. It's also a good idea to think through all the possible questions that Dan the Detective might ask you about your product or service ahead of time, and put the answers in your presentation. You can even provide an FAQ (Frequently Asked Questions) list.

Don't instill doubts in a Detective by describing elaborate pictures of them using your products, like you would do with an Entertainer. Remember, Detectives find excessive enthusiasm suspicious, so to create the strongest bond with them, you want to keep your voice even and matter of fact during the presentation. Never try to sell to a Detective with emotion. Always stick to the facts.

Compare these two scenarios of what works in a presentation to a Detective and what doesn't.

Navigate Role Play: Present to Detectives

Wrong: Jim presents to Dan the Detective as a Fighter.

In their initial meeting, Dan makes it clear to Jim that he wants a house that is going to be the best value for his budget of $350,000.

Jim: Dan, the bottom line is this house gives you the biggest bang for your buck. You need to act fast and move on making a decision. This is not going to stay on the market past today, so I recommend

Chapter 8: Navigate the Presentation

that you go ahead and put in your offer right away.

Dan: You were going to show me a comparative analysis of other homes in the area to determine if this would be the best value.

Jim: Dan, we can go through every analysis you'd like, but I'm telling you, this house has your name written all over it, and if you don't make an offer on it today then there's a good chance you're going to miss out on it.

Dan: *(sharply)* I'm going to check out my options and think about it. Just give me your business card, and I'll give you a call.

Right: Jim adapts his style to a Detective.

Jim: Dan, I did some homework and put together an **analysis** for you. It includes the **details** of several recent **figures** pulled from a cross-section of different locations analyzing the current real estate market in your area. You can see it here on the opposite page of this **spreadsheet**, which includes some **graphs** and **charts**. It also includes a **comparative analysis** of several other homes on the market for you to review. Is this helpful to see?

Dan: Yes, I appreciate the detail here.

Jim: So you can see that when you compare houses in this area with similar specs, this house at $350,000 is the best value. Does that make sense?

Dan: It does.

Jim: And when you look at how the houses in this area have increased in price over the past five years, I believe those numbers will give you confidence that you will achieve your goal to invest in a house that has a track record for steady appreciation. Do you agree?

Dan: I do.

Jim: With your objective to find the best value for your budget of $350,000, can you see how **logical** it is to go with this option?

Dan: Yes, this is very interesting.

Navigate Analysis: In the first scenario, Jim meets with resistance from Dan because he's trying to convince a Detective to make a snap decision without any analytical details to back it up. But in the second scenario, Jim's focus on the details works in his favor. His prepared data is designed to answer Dan's "why" questions before they come up: "Why do I need this product?" "Why is this product better than the competition?" and "Why is this going to save me money?" Even though he shares a lot of detail, Jim organizes it well, and his presentation is still short and to the point despite the amount of information he provides to Dan.

At-a-Glance:
Adapt Your Presentation to Detectives

Do:
- Provide plenty of details
- Use charts, graphs, and figures
- Be specific and objective

Chapter 8: Navigate the Presentation

- Start and end on time
- Answer their "why" questions

Don't:
- Give big-picture generalizations
- Give your opinion
- Sell on emotion
- Force a quick decision

Key Phrases:
- "Here is a spreadsheet with some detailed graphs, figures, and charts and a comparative analysis."
- "Can you see how logical this decision is?"

PRESENT TO COUNSELORS

When you make your presentation to Counselors, you want to focus on the big picture. Explain clearly how your product or service will affect not just Carol the Counselor herself, but her entire team or family. Show her how what you're selling will bring everyone together and make the group stronger at the end of the day. You also want to demonstrate how the purchase will provide stability in the long run, and how it won't disturb the Counselor's current way of life to add it to her ecosystem.

You've already learned that Counselors are not risk takers, and that they generally make slow decisions. That translates to mean that your presentation will take longer with them than it does with any of the other buying behavior styles. Be patient, and remember to check in with them often as you share the benefits of what you're selling.

Here are two role plays that demonstrate the dos and don'ts of presenting to Counselors.

Navigate Role Play: Present to Counselors

Wrong: Jim presents to Carol the Counselor as an Entertainer.

When Jim meets with Carol initially, she shares that her main priority is her family. She would like to be in a safe neighborhood with a great school district.

Jim: Carol, don't you think this house is awesome? I just *love* the unique architecture and how close it is to downtown. Think of all the terrific amenities you'll have access to—and all within walking distance! Can't you just imagine how much fun you'll have living here?

Carol: I'm a little concerned about how close the bars are to the house. As I've mentioned before, my main priority is my children.

Jim: Exactly, which is why I think you're going to love having the movie theater down the street with every restaurant you can desire. The families I talk to tell me they don't mind a little congestion once in a while when they can have access to so much shopping, dining, and entertainment.

Carol: *(crossing her arms)* I don't think this is a fit for my family.

Right: Jim adapts his style to a Counselor.

Jim: So Carol, what I'm going to do is show you a couple of properties, and like I said before, **if you like them, that's great, but if not, it's no big deal**. My favorite clients to work with are couples like you and your husband, who make their families a priority when looking for houses. I met

Chapter 8: Navigate the Presentation

with a couple the other day, and they were telling me that the main thing they look for in a home is a location where their **children can get a great education**. Now, based on what you were telling me earlier, that was a main focus of yours as well. **Is that right?**

Carol: Yes. A nice, **safe neighborhood** in **a good school district** is what we are looking for.

Jim: *(nods)* The two houses in this neighborhood seem to be right up your alley. Their schools have an excellent reputation and can **help provide your kids** with the quality education you're looking for. I think the main reason everyone **feels secure** about choosing our real estate company to work with is that we have so many years of experience developing a superior, full-service company. Southwestern Real Estate is **one of the most dependable companies** in America. How does this sound so far?

Carol: Everything sounds good.

Navigate Analysis: Jim's first presentation makes Carol uncomfortable, because he is trying to sell the excitement of the house when her main concern is actually providing stability for her family.

In the second scenario, he adapts his style to emphasize the long-term benefits to Carol's children. He also makes an emotional connection with Carol by reassuring her about the stability of his company, which helps her to move through the presentation a little more quickly.

At-a-Glance:
Adapt Your Presentation to Counselors

Do:
- Be patient and supportive, and take change gradually
- Ask for their opinion
- Check in often to make sure they understand the product benefits
- Discuss how the group will benefit
- Share company history
- Answer their "how" question

Don't:
- Be demanding
- Focus on what's in it for them instead of their group
- Talk fast
- Force a quick decision

Key Phrases:
- "If you like this, that's great, and if not, it's no big deal."
- "Is that right?" or "Does that make sense?"
- "Your family" or "Your team"

PRESENTATION: NAVIGATED

Now that you understand what Fighters, Entertainers, Detectives, and Counselors value in a presentation, you can put your new knowledge into practice. Prepare four different presentations, one for each style, and practice them until they feel like second nature

Chapter 8: Navigate the Presentation

to you and you find that you're able to switch between them easily. The more comfortable you are with your presentation, the more people you'll be able to serve.

When you adapt to your prospect's needs instead of "showing up and throwing up," you go from hoping something will stick to knowing that you're providing solutions. Better still, you're not delivering just any answers. You're sharing tailored solutions that give real value to the people you're talking to by selling the way they like to buy.

The more value you present to your prospects in the way they want to hear it, the more you'll connect and resonate with them, and the more momentum you'll create for the final step of the sales cycle: the close.

NAVIGATE CASE STUDY:

DAN MOORE

Dan Moore has been the face of Southwestern Advantage™ for more than thirty years, equipping and inspiring salespeople and leaders to perform at their maximum potential.

Early in my sales career, I enjoyed entertaining people. However, as I experienced more success and grew into a leadership role, I recognized that if I wanted to continue to influence people, I was going to need to become a better listener.

I went from being an Entertainer to a Counselor, taking on a more relaxed approach and allowing others to be the star of the show.

Becoming a Counselor helped me create high production levels and synergy in our organization, because people felt that they were listened to and that their opinions were valued and honored. But the Counselor approach did take some adjusting to, especially when it came to working with Fighters. Fighters can come on strong, and it's easy for Counselors to give in to their viewpoints in an effort to keep the peace.

What helped me to work effectively with all the different behavior styles as a Navigator was learning to focus on doing what was best for the whole organization. In other words, push principles over personalities. Even though my natural tendency is to avoid conflict, if the issue concerns a principle we believe in as a company, then I will put my personality aside and get into the conflict that needs to be gotten into. And if the discussion becomes heated, I remind myself, "We all want the same thing. Let me not feel that they're throwing blows at me, personally. They just feel strongly about this."

I've heard it said that Counselors sometimes don't make the best leaders because of their inclination to avoid conflict. But in my experience, I have found that Counselors can be just as strong as Fighters when they remind themselves that it's not about winning the argument. It's about doing what's best for the organization. As the old Tom Peters saying goes, "It doesn't matter who is right. All that matters is what is right."

Chapter 9

NAVIGATE THE CLOSE

DUSTIN NAILS IT: PRACTICE WHAT YOU PREACH

I once presented Southwestern's sales performance consulting program to a group of insurance professionals from Alabama led by a terrific Counselor named Haig. I took everyone through my presentation, and then I went around the table.

"John," I asked, "what are you the most excited about, when it comes to working with Southwestern?" John said that he was most excited about having our coaches work with their sales team. I nodded. Then I looked at Skip and asked, "Skip, you seemed interested in how much thought we put into the research phase of our projects. Is that something you think is a good idea?" Skip told me that, yes, he liked our custom approach.

Then I looked at their leader, Haig. "Haig, I know you're a wise decision maker and would want to talk to your partners before making a decision about this. I have a few emails to check, so I'll step out for a few minutes and let you guys discuss whether this partnership is a fit or not."

"Okay, that sounds good," Haig said.

I got up from the table and headed for the door. Just before I walked through it, I stopped and turned back to the group. "Oh, by the way, we covered all the details there are to talk about today, so the only favor I ask is that you guys just let me know one way or another if this is a fit or not when I come back. Does that sound fair?" I asked.

They all looked at each other and said, "Sure."

I nodded, and I stepped out.

When I walked back in a few minutes later, everyone was laughing.

"What are you laughing about?" I asked.

"We've all read your book, and you just used the 'walk-out close' on us," Haig told me. "We're glad to see you practice what you preach! We're in."

CRAFT THE CLOSE

While the approach gets you in the door, the introduction uncovers the need, and the presentation shows your prospects the value of what you have to offer them, it's the close that actually delivers that value into their hands. You can find the right client, make a connection, demonstrate the benefits that your product has to offer, and still never end up actually serving your prospect at all if you aren't able to Navigate the close.

When people think of closing, they tend to associate the wrong meaning with the word. Many people imagine that closing is about persuading prospects to do something that they don't want to do.

In reality, closing is just the opposite. It's about getting people where they want to go faster. By the time you reach the close, the benefits that your prospects will gain from your product or service are clear. The close is designed to help prospects make the decision that is in their long-term best interests.

You might wonder: Why do people need help acting in their own best interests?

Many people make decisions based on the short-term cost to their wallets instead of focusing on what's really important: their

Chapter 9: Navigate the Close

long-term gain. And many salespeople allow them to do that. The question you need to ask yourself as a Navigator is, are you more concerned with pleasing your prospects or serving them? While pleasing is giving them what they *want*, serving is giving them what they *need*.

As a Navigator, your heart should be in a place of service, and nowhere in the sales cycle does the intention to serve come into play more than in the close. The art of closing is all about Navigating the fear of the buyer. When you understand the different fears of each buying style, you can guide your prospects around those roadblocks to the results and benefits they need.

There is absolutely no reason to feel guilty about this, as long as you are acting from a place of service. What you have to realize is that the prospects you're talking to will most likely get what they need in the end, with or without you. The real question is, will you be the one to serve them, or will it be someone else?

By the time you reach the closing stage of the sales cycle, you will already be in the zone as a Navigator, and you'd think it would be second nature to simply continue matching the buying style of your prospect through the close itself. However, in the heat of the moment before the sale happens, it's easy to forget who you're talking to and lapse back into your natural style of selling.

That's why it's important to stay focused on selling the way people like to buy all the way through the end of the sale. In this chapter, we will teach you exactly how to connect with all four buying behavior styles at this critical point in the sales process.

CLOSE FIGHTERS

By now, you're familiar with the Fighter's greatest fear: *loss of control*. With that in mind, the best way to close a Fighter is a technique called "the choice of two positives."

The choice of two positives is simple, yet very effective with Fighters. You just offer two positive solutions and let Frank the Fighter choose the option that he prefers. This is something you can do all the way through the close. For example, you might say something like, "Which option do you like better, Frank, A or B?" Frank chooses option B, and you continue, "Okay, and would you rather start today or next week?" Frank wants to start next week. "Perfect," you agree, "and would you prefer to pay with a credit card or a check?"

As long as you keep allowing Fighters to stay in control of the situation, they will like and trust you. And with the choice of two positives in your corner, you will do more business with Fighters than you could with any other closing technique out there.

Navigate Role Play: Close Fighters

Wrong: Jim tries to close Frank the Fighter as a Detective.

Jim: Frank, do you have any questions about the statistics and data we have looked at so far?

Frank: Enough with the data. Just tell me how much it is.

Jim: Will do. Let me just share two more statistics. As you can see in this pie chart, 27 percent of the companies that invested in this coaching program saw a 15 percent ROI on their money. And over here on our analysis graph you can see that we have outperformed the competition, based on our proven track record over the course of ten years.

Frank: *(rolls his eyes)* Can we just get to the bottom line? How much is it?

Chapter 9: Navigate the Close

Jim: Well, it depends. We have several different packages. I can show you some statistics so that you can figure out which one is right for you and—

Frank: *(bluntly)* You know what, I don't think I'm interested.

Right: Jim adapts his style to a Fighter.

Jim: So Frank, **which option did you like best, A or B?**

Frank: B.

Jim: What was your favorite feature about option B—**the price or the convenience?**

Frank: The price!

Jim: *(pulls out the contract)* Okay, well, if I'm reading you right, it seems like this package is the best fit for you. All I need to know to get you started is whether you get your mail at **your house or the office?**

Navigate Analysis: Jim loses the sale in the first role play because he crosses the buying line and reviews too much detail with his cut-to-the-chase Fighter. That destroys his momentum, and Frank loses interest. In the second scenario, Jim moves directly to the close once he knows that Frank is on board. He closes using the choice of two positives, which keeps Frank in control of the buying experience to the end.

At-a-Glance:
Adapt Your Close to Fighters

Do:
- Move to the close as soon as they're on board
- Cut to the chase
- Use the choice of two positives

Don't:
- Sell past the buying line
- Give them fewer than two choices

Key Phrases:
- "Which option do you like best, A or B?"

CLOSE ENTERTAINERS

With the Entertainer's greatest fear being *rejection*, this translates into doubt as to whether or not she'll "look cool" when it comes to the close. The most effective way to bring Emily the Entertainer to a point of decision is to help her dream about what owning your product or service will be like, so that she can experience how much she'll love it in advance and gain the confidence she needs to move forward.

With that in mind, a great technique to use with Entertainers is the "crystal ball" close. The crystal ball close builds on the discovery process you went through with the Entertainer during your introduction, when you started to help her dream about her ideal product or service. With the crystal ball close, you forecast the Entertainer's future and invite her to specifically visualize the benefits that your product will ultimately leave her with. This is the boost of excitement the Entertainer needs to cross the buying line.

Chapter 9: Navigate the Close

For example, if you were selling a car to an Entertainer, you might say, "Emily, five years from now, what do you see yourself enjoying most about this car? Do you see yourself with the convertible top down and your hair blowing in the wind, going down the freeway? Do you see your friends piled in, jamming out to some tunes on this awesome Bose stereo system?" Emily experiences an emotional charge from imagining herself in the picture you painted for her, and that translates into a sale.

Navigate Role Play: Close Entertainers

Wrong: Jim tries to close Emily the Entertainer as a Counselor.

Jim: Emily, what do you like best about the coaching program so far? How it will help free up some of your time to work on big-picture strategy? What's the impact it will have on the team?

Emily: This would make my life a lot more enjoyable, not having to spend all my time training our team!

Jim: Good. As I mentioned at the beginning, if you decide to move forward with this, great, and if not, that's okay too. Sound good?

Emily: That's fine. I do think the coaching would be great.

Jim: Good. Now Emily, what do you think your team will think about the coaching program?

Emily: That's a good question. I guess I'd better check in with them first and get back to you. Can I have your card please?

Jim: Of course. Here's my card. Give me a call after you speak with them.

Right: Jim adapts his style to an Entertainer.

Jim: Well, Emily, it seems like this coaching program is going to be a terrific fit for your team. I really think they're going to be **pumped up** to hear about how coaching will take their business to the next level! As a matter of fact, the other day I was **talking with Amanda** from the Franklin office, and she was telling me about **how exciting** coaching has been for her. She told me that if she could have flashed forward one year into the future and known that she would be making twice the amount of money *while* having more time with her family and **having fun**, she never would have second-guessed signing up for coaching. She told me that hiring a coach from Southwestern was the best decision she's ever made!

Emily: Wow! That sounds great!

Jim: **Just imagine one year from now: your team has gone through the coaching program** and they are running on all cylinders, being proactive with their schedules and time. What do you think the overall picture of the company would look like with everyone in coaching for a year and **at the top of their game**?

Emily: I think the picture of the company would look awesome!

Jim: That's exactly right! So, let's get them all set up!

Emily: Let's do it!

Navigate Analysis: In the first scenario, Jim asks Emily the

Chapter 9: Navigate the Close

worst closing question on earth: "What do you think your team will think about the coaching program?" That question inevitably evokes the response, "I don't know. Let me talk to my team about it." In the second conversation, however, Jim closes using enthusiasm, selling the experience of the coaching program and telling Emily a fun story about one of her friends. His crystal ball close lets her mentally experience the results of having a sales coach, and that moves her across the buying line.

At-a-Glance: Adapt Your Close to Entertainers

Do:
- Speak with enthusiasm
- Tell stories about friends who purchased the product or service
- Use the crystal ball close

Don't:
- Forget to paint the big picture
- Ask, "What do you think?"

Key Phrases:
- "What do you see yourself enjoying most about this?"
- "Can you see yourself . . ."

CLOSE DETECTIVES

Because a Detective's biggest fear is making a mistake, emotional strategies such as the crystal ball approach are the worst thing you can throw at them during the close. Detectives don't trust emotions. In their minds, emotional decisions lead to mistakes. They think logically, and they want to buy logically, based on the facts. Considering this, the best logical closing technique to use with Detectives is the "product, price, performance" close, aka the PPP close.

The PPP close is designed to eliminate the possibility of mistakes in the decision-making process. It simply asks Dan the Detective three questions, followed by a direct closing statement. The three questions are "Do you like the product and think it is something that you will use?" "Based on the value you are receiving, do you think the investment (price) is fair?" and "Based on everything we have discussed, do you believe and trust me to deliver on the services I've promised to perform?"

After Dan the Detective confirms "yes" to all three logical closing questions, you then direct close him with, "Dan, this just seems to make sense. You should do this; it should be a no-brainer. Moving forward seems like the logical thing to do, wouldn't you agree?" The PPP close leaves no stone unturned and confirms to the Detective that he has in fact logically analyzed the product or service from every angle, at which point he realizes that he's ready to move forward.

When you can logically walk Detectives through the product, price, and performance of your offering, you will consistently and unemotionally be able to close deals with them. The PPP close is organized, informative, and to the point—just what Detectives like.

Navigate Role Play: Close Detectives

Wrong: Jim tries to close Dan the Detective as an Entertainer.

Jim: Dan, if you could look into a crystal ball and see five years into the future, what would you see your team enjoying the most about this coaching

Chapter 9: Navigate the Close

program? Would they be most excited to have experienced coaches in their corner to help them power through the hard days? Would they enjoy having somebody help them with their process to convert more dials into appointments set?

Dan: I'm not sure what they'd like most, but what I'm really more concerned with is the ROI we'd receive.

Jim: I can tell you firsthand, your team will definitely get an ROI. Our coaches are great about helping clients to be fearless on the phone, which of course is going to lead to higher production.

Dan: I'm not comfortable making an investment in a program that doesn't have proof that it works.

Jim: You're welcome to call any of our clients and talk to them about their results.

Dan: Okay, please give me a list of your clients, and then I'll get back to you.

Right: Jim adapts his style to a Detective.

Jim: Dan, as we talked about earlier, the average client in our program increases production by 23 percent after the first six months. With this said, do you **logically** see how having a coach hold your team accountable will help them reach their goals?

Dan: Yes.

Jim: Great. Now Dan, I remember you saying that with **the value you are receiving compared** with everything else on the market, you thought **the investment was reasonable** for this program. Do you agree that **the investment is fair**?

Dan: Yes, the investment seems fair.

Jim: Okay. Based on our conversation so far, do you believe that I will follow through in providing you a quality experience and trust that I will do everything I said I would do to get you set up in the program?

Dan: Yes. I trust you.

Jim: *(looks Dan square in the eyes)* You know, Dan, this just seems to **make sense. You should do this.** This should be a **no-brainer**. Moving forward seems like the **logical** thing to do, wouldn't you agree?

Dan: I agree.

Navigate Analysis: Jim's crystal ball close in the first role play is too much for Dan, who isn't interested in dreaming about the coaching program and who just wants to get back to the details and fundamentals of the service.

In the second scenario, Jim earns the sale by covering all of Dan's main objections and Navigating the Detective through the PPP close. After going through the PPP, Dan's lingering concerns about the program are alleviated, and he's ready to make a deal.

Chapter 9: Navigate the Close

At-a-Glance:
Adapt Your Close to Detectives

Do:
- Speak with an even tone of voice
- Use logic, facts, and details
- Use the PPP close

Don't:
- Be too enthusiastic or emotional
- Forget to address their concerns

Key Phrases:
- "Do you see the value of this product?"
- "Do you think the price is fair?"
- "Do you believe I will deliver for you on what I've said?"

CLOSE COUNSELORS

As you've seen in earlier chapters, a Counselor's greatest fear is *change*. If change has to happen at all, Counselors want it to happen gradually, with as little disruption to their lives as possible. They make decisions through consensus, in part because they feel a sense of safety and stability in numbers, and you need to take the group element into account when you Navigate a Counselor through the close. With that in mind, a great technique to use with Counselors is the "walk-out" close.

Counselors usually tell you that they need to discuss your product or service with their team or partner before making a decision. The walk-out close takes that objection and allows you to use it to your advantage. Before you use the walk-out close, you reiterate the selling points of your presentation in a way that shows them the great improvements with minor disruptions that you are offering, and you make sure that every member of the team is on the same page. Then you leave the room and return a few minutes later, after Carol the Counselor has had time to discuss the decision with her team—just as Dustin did with the insurance team from Alabama.

Here are the four steps to the walk-out close:

Plant positive seeds. Ask the influencers what they liked best.

Ask for the exit. Stand up and say, "I'm going to step outside for a few seconds to give you time to discuss this without me in the room."

Ask for an answer today. As you are walking out the door, say, "The only favor I ask is when I come back in let me know one way or another, yes or no."

Walk outside and pray!

Always make sure you ask the Counselor and her team to give you a yes or no answer, in a low-pressure way, before you perform the walk-out close. When you do this, you can head off "maybes" at the pass and help the Counselor move forward with confidence.

Navigate Role Play: Close Counselors

Wrong: Jim tries to close Carol the Counselor as a Fighter.

Jim speaks to Carol and her team.

Jim: Carol, Bill, and Susan, bottom line, can you see how this will blow up your production?

Chapter 9: Navigate the Close

Carol: It certainly has promise, but we've never done anything like this before, so we're going to need to think about it.

Jim: I understand how you feel. We've had clients who have felt the same way. What they realized, however, is that if they don't push themselves out of their comfort zone, they never have the opportunity to crush their production. To get started, I just need to get your mailing address. Do you get your mail at work or the post office?

Carol: We appreciate your presentation. We never make a decision on the spot, and we're going to need time to talk it over and think about it. We'll give you a call sometime next week.

Jim: I understand what you're saying, but here's something to consider. If the team members continue to do what they're doing, they're going to continue to get the same results. With this program, however, it's an opportunity to grow their production. If that makes sense, what do you say we go ahead and get started?

Carol: I really don't feel comfortable about this. I think we're fine with what we've got. I appreciate you taking the time with us today. Feel free to check back with us in twelve months.

Right: Jim adapts his style to a Counselor.

Jim: You know, Carol, **if I'm reading you right**, you seem to think this is a pretty good idea. Based on what I'm hearing, **everyone seems to like** the benefits and features. Susan, what **resonated with you** in the presentation?

Susan: I really like that this program saves us money.

Jim: Okay. And Bill, what was **your favorite part**?

Bill: I really think this will help the team work more effectively.

Jim: Well, Carol, I know you are a **wise decision maker** and that all of you probably **want to discuss this together as a team**. I want to make sure that you have the opportunity to discuss it without me in the room, so **I'm going to step out** for five minutes and check a few emails. We've covered everything about the program, how it works, and what solutions it provides your team, so **by this point we've discussed all the details and you guys should know if this is right for you or not**. The important thing is to make sure you are all on the same page. **Whatever you decide is fine by me. The only favor that I ask is that you give me a yes or a no when I return. Does that sound fair?**

Carol: I was just about to ask you for your card and tell you that we'd call you next week, after we discussed it as a team. But now that you mention it, a few minutes alone is really all we need to see if this is something we want to move forward with. Thank you, that sounds like a great idea.

Jim walks out of the room for five minutes and returns five minutes later to find that Carol and her team are ready to move forward.

Navigate Analysis: In the first scenario, Jim loses the sale because his assumptive close puts too much pressure on Carol, who becomes uncomfortable and decides to pass. But in the

Chapter 9: Navigate the Close

second dialogue, Jim picks up on Carol's discomfort and Navigates it, creating a buying environment by making sure that the team is on the same page and then using the walk-out close. The low pressure and team consensus take Carol to the buying line, and Jim is able to close the sale that same day.

Groups can be difficult if you don't handle them right, because the different team members tend to play off of one another, and in the end they decide that they need to "get back to you" with an answer—which is much less likely to be a "yes" after you leave. That's why it's much better to make the sale happen the same day. The walk-out close always improves your chances of closing a Counselor and her team on the first meeting.

At-a-Glance:
Adapt Your Close to Counselors

Do:
- Take the pressure off
- Emphasize benefits and downplay disruptions
- Get the team on the same page
- Use the walk-out close

Don't:
- Try to force a decision
- Dwell on radical change
- Neglect to give the team alone time to discuss

Key Phrases:
- "I know you're a wise decision maker."
- "You probably want to discuss this together as a team."

CLOSE WITH CONFIDENCE

As a salesperson, it's easy to hear a "yes" at the close of the sales cycle, and you can live with a "no," but it's the "maybes" that kill you. Worse, those "maybes" are a disservice to your prospects, who deserve the better quality of life that your product or service can give them. When you learn to Navigate the close for all four buying styles, you save yourself the anguish of hearing people tell you "maybe," and you serve your clients the way they should be served.

Just as you prepared four presentations to fit each of the different buying styles, you should also prepare four closes. Being prepared ahead of time will help you roll with the punches more easily in those unpredictable moments.

But here's some good news: at this stage in your *Navigate* training, those unpredictable moments are few and far between.

You now know how to Navigate the sales cycle from start to finish. That makes you a bona-fide Navigator on your way to becoming a top producer. Keep in mind that practice makes perfect, and you'll want to frequently refer to the guidelines we've just covered until you become comfortable with them.

But even after you master the basics of Navigating, as a student of the game, you know that the learning process never truly ends. There's never a final destination to the art of selling the way people like to buy, and you can always go deeper. In the next chapter, we'll partner with you to Navigate the really tough ones, equipping you with tools to take your *Navigate* skills to even greater heights.

> **TIP-OFF**
>
> For free sales training tips, join Dustin's blog at http://sellingtheway peopleliketobuy.com/

Chapter 9: Navigate the Close

NAVIGATE CASE STUDY:

MARK DUGGER

Mark Dugger is the director of the National Contact Center for Cellular Sales and leads the nation's largest and fastest-growing Verizon Wireless retailer.

I'm in an industry where technology is constantly changing, and in order to continue to stay on top, I've got to aggressively lead the charge. My Fighter tendency enables me to do whatever it takes to move the ship forward. But while my tenacious style has served me over the years, as I continued to grow in my leadership, I became aware that I could be a little too aggressive.

One of my biggest struggles was working with the IT department. I was so focused on getting the job done that I'd find myself plowing through without thinking about my teammates' behavior style preferences. I wanted to speed things up, but in the end I'd slow them down by not providing the detail the Detectives desired or the consensus the Counselors needed or the rapport the Entertainers thrived on. I realized that I had to learn to control my Fighter tendencies if I was going to grow as a high-impact leader.

Navigate's breakdown of each behavior style and its specific instructions on how to adapt to each of them made a lot of sense to me. I started putting its principles into play and worked on exerting more patience before moving forward. I reminded myself to actively watch and listen to the pressing needs of other individuals. Ever since, I've been seeing an atmosphere where the walls come down, trust increases, and real, healthy communication is able to take place. I've been able to connect with my team on a more meaningful level.

Navigate not only has helped in my communication with others, but also has helped our team to communicate better as a whole. Those who have embraced this skill have moved up the ladder faster. These *Navigate* skills are some of the most crucial tools for success, in both one's professional and one's personal life.

Chapter 10

NAVIGATE THE TOUGH ONES

STEVE TRADES PRIDE FOR HUMILITY

Becoming a Navigator wasn't easy for me. I spent a lot of years determined to do things my way. I was out to prove that I was right, and others were wrong.

Of course, you can imagine what that got me: a lot of broken relationships.

I finally reached my pain threshold and realized, "Something needs to change—in me." And I became determined to figure out what it was. I embraced the pain I felt and leveraged it to push me to where I needed to be. My purpose was to learn how to work effectively with others, regardless of how they were treating me.

I traded in my pride for humility. And that was where the *Navigate* shift happened.

Once I became a Navigator, I started to appreciate people's differences. My peace of mind and success both increased, because I was focused on the Platinum Rule. I was more concerned with serving than with selling. And I connected with—and sold to—more people from all walks of life than ever before.

My journey didn't end once I'd learned to Navigate the different styles. It still hasn't ended. Every day, I learn more about how to bring out the best in people, help them fearlessly pursue their goals, and inspire them to a life of significance in serving others. You will, too.

This chapter will arm you with tools to Navigate even the tough ones so that you can take the art of selling the way people like to buy to a new level of mastery.

NAVIGATE CROSS QUADRANTS

The truth is, if you've gotten this far in the *Navigate* system, you've already started to put the concept of Navigating cross quadrants into practice. When we talk about cross quadrants, we're talking about learning to connect with the buying behavior style that is the polar opposite of your natural selling style. You probably already know which style is the hardest for you to adapt to intuitively. But let's break down the key characteristics that cause the rift.

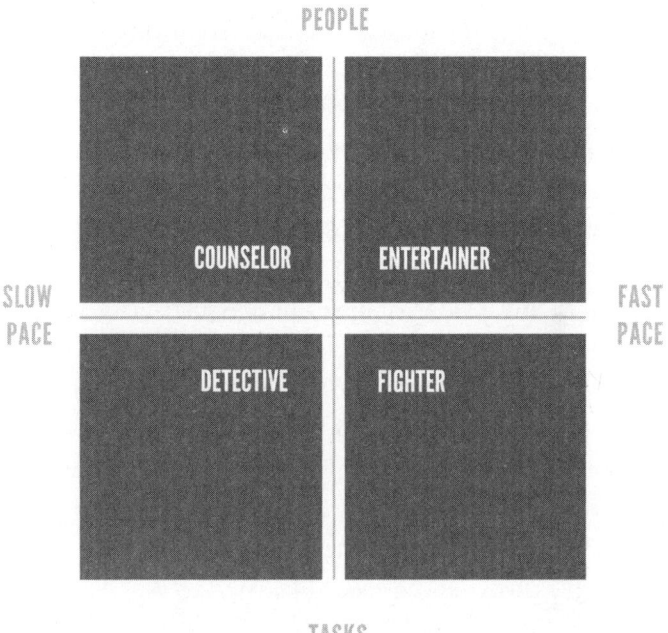

Chapter 10: Navigate the Tough Ones

As you can see in diagram 10.1, we define the four *Navigate* styles based on their preference for tasks or people, and their tendency to make fast or slow decisions. Fighters prefer tasks and make fast decisions. Entertainers also make fast decisions, but they gravitate toward people more than tasks. Counselors are people-focused, slow decision makers, and Detectives are slow decision makers who prefer tasks.

Typically, the hardest buying style for you to adapt to is the one at the opposite end of your cross quadrant. For example, if you're a Fighter by nature, Navigating Counselors will be your biggest challenge. If you're a Detective, Entertainers will drive you up the wall—and vice versa.

When you first begin Navigating, it may feel like you're never going to be able to connect with your cross-quadrant buying style. You have some common ground with the other two, but that cross-quadrant buyer probably feels about as alien to you as another human can get. So what can you do to help yourself get in the swing of Navigating cross quadrants?

You can focus on the personal growth opportunities that relate directly to your cross-quadrant buying style. And you can work to understand the deeper psychology of why your opposite is the way he or she is to help you find common ground.

But Those Fighters Are So Argumentative, Bull Headed, and Rude

If you're a Counselor by nature, learning to work with Fighters will be your biggest challenge as a Navigator. They can come across abrasively, without question. But here's a new perspective to consider: Fighters don't generally attack people to be malicious.

In fact, Fighters can often end up feeling bad about attacking people at all. Because their nature is to be so results oriented, they can sometimes get stressed when things don't go according to plan. This occasionally results in a knee-jerk reaction, and they say things they may regret later. As a Counselor, rather than taking their attacks personally, your growth opportunity is to have compassion for whatever the secret cause of your Fighter-buyer's "negative behavior" may be. Otherwise, it's like getting upset with a person who has a broken leg for lagging behind the group.

When you learn not to take the abruptness of Fighters personally, you're actually strengthening your emotional muscles. You're learning to be hard to offend, and quick to forgive and forget. You're learning to roll with the punches. And that's going to make you a better Navigator in the long run.

A good reminder to tell yourself when dealing with a Fighter is "It's not about me." And rather than basing your self-worth on what the prospect says to you, draw your confidence from knowing at your core that you're a servant salesperson. Once you learn to Navigate Frank the Fighter's attacks, don't be surprised when—after you cut to the chase and satisfy his need to get to the *bottom line*—he transforms from an aggressive Fighter into a warm teddy bear!

I Don't Think I Can Handle One More Loud-Mouthed, Annoying, Inconsistent Entertainer

If you're a Detective, this sentiment probably sounds familiar. Entertainers can really get to you with their focus on subjective dreams and incessant brainstorming, instead of looking at the real, concrete facts right in front of their noses. And there's nothing worse than an Entertainer who tells you that her team is *definitely* going to buy what you're selling and then drops off the face of the planet without a whisper.

But here's what's going on behind the scenes:

Emily the Entertainer really meant it when she told you that her team would be interested in your product. But when she went back to tell her Fighter-Detective boss about it, she couldn't

Chapter 10: Navigate the Tough Ones

remember any of the details, and he or she shot the idea down. Entertainers are so sensitive to what people think of them that the last thing Emily wants to do is disappoint you, the salesperson she looked in the eye and said, "Yes, we want it! You can count on our partnership." So rather than let you down, she doesn't call you, and she stops returning your voicemails.

With this in mind, you'll want to practice acceptance when you're dealing with Entertainers. Instead of grinding your teeth when they go on and on about the people they know, try to appreciate their zest for life.

A great strategy to use with Entertainers is to not allow yourself to get too excited by their excitement. Instead, remain calm and devise a plan to head off their roller-coaster experience of emotions. Try to help Entertainers come up with a realistic game plan for what *really* needs to happen to form this partnership: Who are the decision makers, what will be the criteria for making the decision, and what is the timeline?

Because Entertainers tend to miss a lot of the details, ideally you'll want to schedule a meeting for you to present to others in their organization. At the very least, you'll want to go through a dress rehearsal with the Entertainer for how he or she will present your product to other people. Make sure the Entertainer is equipped with all the details he or she needs to score a touchdown.

Those Skeptical, Anal, Pessimistic Detectives Make Me Crazy

Just as Entertainers drive Detectives crazy, if you're an Entertainer, then Detective-buyers can really get under your skin. They need so many facts and speak with so little emotion that you start to wonder if there's a real human in there, or if you're secretly talking to a robot.

A new way to look at this is that Detectives aren't actually pessimists; they're realists. When Detective Dan sits and looks over the numbers with a frown on his face and his eyebrows furrowed, he's not necessarily unhappy, and he's not being critical of *you*. He's just analyzing the facts. There's no need to take it personally.

Still, as an Entertainer, you might find that Detectives zap your energy, regardless of whether they mean to. So how do you deal with that?

The growth opportunity is to learn to be a thermostat instead of a thermometer. While a thermometer *reflects* the temperature of the environment, a thermostat *sets* it. When you become a thermostat, it doesn't matter what kind of skepticism a Detective or anyone else throws at you. Because while as a thermometer you might allow a Detective's critical nature to derail you, as a thermostat you predetermine your outlook, and you're prepared to roll with the punches. Your attitude is, "While I can't control others, I can always control my response to them."

With this in mind, when you find yourself with a Detective, you no longer have to try to get *through* the criticism. Instead, you can actually *embrace* it as you appreciate Dan the Detective's need for details and simply provide them to him. And that makes you a stronger Navigator.

If This Counselor Moves Any Slower, I'm Going to Lose My Mind

Counselors may seem thoughtful and kind to everyone else. But if you're a Fighter, this buying behavior style frustrates you more than any other. You just can't wrap your head around how these people can possibly take so long to make a decision about something that's clearly good for them. They seem downright spineless, sometimes.

But at the end of the day, Counselors are really just trying to accomplish the same thing you are: making the best decision

Chapter 10: Navigate the Tough Ones

for all parties involved. In fact, you have to admire how selfless Counselors are, how they tend to put the needs of others above themselves. So rather than let their methodical process make you *impatient*, think of it as a growth opportunity to make yourself *more patient*.

So learn to be okay with taking the pressure off of Carol the Counselor when you're serving her. Create a buying atmosphere where you say, "My goal is to serve you regardless of whether we partner together. If you decide to move forward, great. If not, that's okay too. Sound fair?" If you cultivate patience with your Counselors, they will be drawn to your relaxed, service-minded attitude, and they'll actually move a little faster than if you were trying to drag them along for the ride.

NAVIGATE SAME QUADRANTS

At first glance, Navigating prospects who fall into the same quadrant as you might appear to be the *easiest* style for you to work with. If there's one buying style you truly feel comfortable with, it's your own, right? Yet while this might be true, it's also the style that can present you with the biggest pitfalls. Precisely *because* you feel so comfortable around somebody who shares your style, you may find a tendency to actually do the *least* amount of Navigating compared to the other styles. How can this be?

Here's the key: *Navigating is not mirroring.*

People often mistake Navigating for mirroring, but it's not the same thing. Whereas mirroring is duplicating another person's style, Navigating is knowing how to best serve your prospects by understanding how they make decisions and adapting your style accordingly. For example, if you put two Entertainers in a room together, while you might have a fun time mirroring each other (swapping stories and laughing a lot), you might never end up doing business together if you don't Navigate, because you'll never get to the bottom line.

Navigating is actually the *least* natural thing to do when you're with somebody who shares your behavior style. Here are some key things to remember about Navigating same quadrants.

Fighters Butt Heads

Have you ever seen two Fighters going head to head, toe to toe? It's not a pleasant sight.

With two Fighters, things can get ugly—and fast. Think about that time you were behind in your production and you were determined to make that next sale. You were encouraged when you figured out that your prospect was also a Fighter, because he told you that he was short on time and actually *wanted* you to cut to the chase. *No problem*, you told yourself as you picked up your pace and hit him with the bottom line for how your product would influence his business. When he told you he already had a provider that he was happy with, you ate that objection for breakfast as you explained what made your product superior.

You were so confident in your approach that it shocked you when you went to close him and he told you he wasn't interested. Trying not to let it faze you, you hit him with your assumptive close and were even more shocked when he escorted you out the door. As you slammed your car in reverse, frustrated and feeling like you just got out of a brawl, you wondered: *What in the world went wrong?*

Your first problem in that scenario was thinking that it was a good idea to try to *overcome* your Fighter-buyer's objection that he already had a provider he was happy with by telling him why your product was better. That's like trying to put your fist through a brick wall. Remember this from chapter 4? It doesn't work because you're basically telling the potentially prideful Fighter that he made a poor decision going with his provider. And if that wasn't bad enough, when he told you he wasn't interested and you came right back at him with another closing statement, it didn't work because stubborn Frank the Fighter will never allow himself to be "closed."

Yet as a Fighter-seller, this is exactly how you'll feel inclined to approach your Fighter-buyers.

If you're tired of butting heads with other Fighters, the first thing you want to remember is to check your pride at the door. Let your Fighter prospect have some control. Rather than trying to *overcome* his objection with a *statement*, you want to *embrace* his objection with *questions*: "Tell me about your current provider. What do you like best about them? Now if you could take their service to the next level, what would you like to be different? If I can share how my product can continue to provide what you like (list what he likes) while improving what you'd like to be different (list what he'd like to alter), would this be something you'd be serious about moving forward on?"

The more Frank the Fighter feels like you're trying to tell him what to do, the more he's going to fight you on it. On the other hand, the more you can get him to come up with the solution himself, the more buy-in he's going to have. With this in mind, keep your own Fighter instincts on a tight leash, and *never tell what you can ask*. Remember, Frank will believe only a little of what you say. He'll believe a little more if it comes from a third-party testimonial. However, he'll buy in most if he feels like the answer is coming from himself.

When the Wrong Entertainer Is the Star of the Show

Now, you might be thinking, "Okay, I can understand how two Fighters going head to head would be a bad thing, but what could possibly go wrong with two Entertainers having fun together?"

Well, because Entertainers love to visualize things, check out this vision:

You walk into your Entertainer-buyer's office, and it's loaded with fun. Emily the Entertainer has a golf bag in one corner and fishing poles in the other. She's got uplifting quotes all over her walls. But what really catch your eye are the pictures of her in Hawaii with her friends and family covering her desk. After a jovial greeting, you have no doubt that you are with an Entertainer. Let the games begin.

Knowing that Entertainers want to do business with people they like, you hone in on the Hawaii pictures right away and mention that Hawaii is your favorite place to take your family. In fact, you go on for the next fifteen minutes sharing stories of all the fun experiences you have had on your Hawaii getaways.

Everything seems to be going according to plan as you get into your presentation and continue to impress Emily with story after story about how awesome your product is. Things take a turn for the worse, however, when she suddenly looks at her watch and realizes she's late for her next appointment. She tells you she's really enjoyed meeting you and asks you to call next week. Three weeks go by, however, and you can't understand why Emily the Entertainer has still not returned your calls.

What happened in this case is that the wrong person tried to be the star of the show. While it's true that Entertainers like to entertain, if you're the salesperson, that means you want to get *your prospect* to do most of the talking—not the other way around! When you as an Entertainer saw the pictures of Hawaii on Emily's desk, it would have been a great opportunity to ask her about her trip. When you get Emily the Entertainer talking about something she's passionate about, you've gained instant likeability, which is critical because Entertainers want to do business with people they enjoy being with. However, when you end up making yourself the center of attention, it can actually frustrate the Entertainer prospect, who feels that this salesperson is just full of him- or herself. With this in mind, as an Entertainer-seller attempting to engage with an Entertainer-buyer, a good rule to remember is "Focus on being *interested* rather than on being *interesting*."

The other obvious challenge when you get two Entertainers

Chapter 10: Navigate the Tough Ones

together is how easy it is to lose track of time. The problem here is twofold. First, you don't give yourself enough time to close the sale, and second, you leave your Entertainer-buyer thinking, "This guy is a lot of fun, but while I might like him as a friend, he's probably not the person I'm going to trust to do business with." That said, as an Entertainer-seller, as soon as you realize that you're with another Entertainer, you need to remind yourself that there's a good chance your prospect might go off on tangents, and it's your job to reel him or her back in. By effectively managing Emily the Entertainer's time and attention, in addition to getting her to like you, you'll earn her respect and confidence.

When Too Many Details Bog Down the Detective

If you're a Detective, you might be thinking, "All right, I get how two Fighters can clash and I completely understand two Entertainers not being able to do business together, but I don't see *why* there would be an issue with two Detectives working together."

Well, let's process this.

Let's say you enter a sales interaction and conclude right away that your prospect is a Detective by all the detailed questions he asks you. You feel right at home, because details are your middle name. Without hesitation, you answer every question with charts, graphs, and tables. For every objection Dan the Detective throws at you, you steer clear of giving any opinions and stick entirely to facts, figures, and written documentation. When you attempt to close the sale, you're not at all surprised when he tells you he needs to think about it. After all, if you were to put yourself in his shoes, you would do the exact same thing. You even pride yourself on not making snap decisions and always doing your due diligence. With this in mind, you tell Dan to take all the time he needs.

What you can't understand, however, is why every time you call to follow up with him, he continues to say he needs more time to think about it, to process it, to weigh the pros and cons. So what went wrong?

It's true that Detectives want details and time to process everything. The problem, however, is that because Detectives are perfectionists, they might never be able to do enough research to be able to guarantee that your product is beyond a doubt the perfect solution for their needs. As we shared in chapter 3, because their biggest fear is making a mistake, they will overthink, overprocess, and overanalyze to the point of giving themselves paralysis by analysis, in which they are never able to make a decision.

As a salesperson, if you're not able to take your Detective cap off, you'll just continue to feed your prospect's procrastination, empathizing with his need to make the perfect decision and ultimately resulting in him making no decision at all.

So what's the solution?

Understanding your own tendency to overanalyze, you need to come to the realization that *done is better than perfect*. This doesn't mean that you skip your due diligence entirely. Rather, it's about having both a process to help you make a decision and the confidence to move forward before it's too late. It's about recognizing that you're not serving your prospect by enabling him to put his life on hold through procrastination. It's about understanding that if you leave it to your prospect to make a decision, it will be painstakingly slow and might not ever happen. Therefore, it's your job to help him make the best decision he can.

It's been said that Detectives don't buy on emotion, but that's not entirely true. After all, we just finished discussing how it's next to impossible to "logically" make the "perfect" decision. With this in mind, making a good decision often involves connecting with one's *heart* as well as one's *head*. Therefore, as a Detective, you'll want to recognize your growth opportunity to add *emotion* to your sales process not just with your Entertainers, Counselors, and Fighters, but with your Detectives as well.

Chapter 10: Navigate the Tough Ones

Here's an example. When Dan the Detective tells you he needs more time to think about it (after you've already loaded him down with details), you reply, "Dan, can I have permission to be completely transparent?" (Of course.) "If you were my own brother, this is what I would tell you: You shared that once you had all of the details on the program you would make a decision. Even after you received those details, you felt you needed even more of them. Then, once you received those additional details, you said you needed two more weeks to make a decision. Now, today, you're telling me you still can't make a decision and you'll need another two weeks. Dan, if you were my own brother, do you know what I would say to you?" (What would you say?) "What do you think I would say?" (You'd say I need to stop procrastinating and just do it.) "Why do you think I'd say that?" (Because I keep putting this off for no good reason.) "You got it. So what do you say we stop putting this off and make it happen?" (Absolutely.) "Great."

Bottom line? If you're a Detective, you have the knowledge to become a solid salesperson. And when you learn to combine your logical side with emotion, you'll become a terrific Navigator.

Counselors Can Be Too Accommodating

If there's one style that seems most likely to work well together, it's the Counselors. After all, Counselors are so accommodating. They're team players; their desire is to please, and they put others' needs above their own. So what's the problem with two Counselors doing business together?

Consider this scenario.

You sit down in your prospect's office, and right away Carol the Counselor makes you feel comfortable by offering you a cup of coffee, tea, soda, juice, or water. She comes around her desk and offers you a seat on the sofa as she sits in the chair across from you. You feel right at home, relieved to know that you're with another

Counselor. As a wealth management advisor, your job is to get to know your prospect.

So you ask Carol questions about her hobbies, family, and financial goals. She shares with you that she'd like to pay for her children's college and retire by age sixty-five. When you ask her what investments she's made for the future, she looks down and says, "Nothing as of yet." When you ask her if she'd be interested in seeing a plan to achieve her goals, she smiles and says she'd like that. You shake hands and agree to meet again in a week.

A week later, when you present a proposal to get Carol on track for paying for her children's college and retirement, she thanks you for the work you've put into the plan but says that she and her husband have decided to hold off on doing anything for another year. Determined not to say anything that might offend her, you politely ask what caused her to change her mind. She explains that the timing is not right as they've had unforeseen expenses come up, but she assures you that next year they'll be in a better spot. Discouraged that you've lost the sale but understanding Carol's situation, you thank her for her time and promise to follow up with her in twelve months.

When you sit down with your sales manager for your weekly conference and he asks you how you're doing, you share with him all of the great relationships you've been developing and all of the promising opportunities you have in your pipeline. He reviews your list and can't help but show his displeasure as he notices that the same names have been there for several months. He asks you if you're familiar with the term "professional visitor."

If you're a Counselor, you're probably all too familiar with this experience. While Fighters can get under your skin, you appreciate how they at least make decisions. While Detectives can make your head spin with all their questions, it's nice how once they see all the details, they eventually see the logic in moving forward.

Chapter 10: Navigate the Tough Ones

While Entertainers can talk your ear off, you like how once they visualize the big picture, they buy. Other Counselors, however, can actually be your toughest sale. They are uncomfortable with change, everything must meet with their spouse's approval, and the last thing you want to do is create waves. Your feeling is that you got into sales to help people, and if Carol the Counselor does not want to move forward, then who are you to try to push her to do so?

While as a laid-back Counselor salesperson you feel conviction in your mission to help people, what you don't necessarily realize is the difference between pleasing and serving. While pleasing is giving the prospects what they *want*, serving is giving them what they *need*. Although Carol the Counselor might not *want* to change her budget to invest in a financial product, it might be exactly what she *needs* to do in order to achieve her family's financial goals. Your growth opportunity is to remember that your job is not to please people but to serve them. That involves helping people make the best decisions for their families long term. In order to do so, you have to be willing to get out of your own comfort zone to best serve your prospects.

You have to be willing to discuss pain.

Often, people will not change their behavior until the pain of *not changing* is greater than the pain of *changing*. For example, when Carol the Counselor says it's not in her budget to invest in her retirement, she's basically saying she's uncomfortable with changing her budget. She enjoys taking her family to the movies and restaurants on the weekends. She's afraid if she invests in her retirement she might not be able to continue to do the things she's used to doing. The bottom line is that she's uncomfortable with changing her behavior.

However, if you as the Counselor-seller get Carol the Counselor thinking about the pain of *not changing* her behavior, it changes everything. In other words, if you can get her thinking about the pain she will feel in not being able to achieve her retirement goals, that unpleasant future suddenly becomes the greater pain—and that's when people change their behavior.

Here's an example of how this plays out.

Carol the Counselor tells you that it's not in her budget to invest in her retirement because of sudden car expenses. You tell Carol that you understand how she feels and say that you want what's best for her family long term. With that in mind, you ask her for permission to be completely transparent, and because you've earned her trust, she agrees. "I understand it will be uncomfortable to rearrange the budget to make this investment, Carol," you say, "but let me ask you this question: How uncomfortable will it be not to be able to retire with your husband at age sixty-five? What would it mean to your family if you had to continue to work? How will you feel about not being able to do the kind of traveling you were planning on doing when you retire?"

As you get your prospect to consider the long-term pain of *not changing*, she suddenly becomes ready to make the change. And this approach fits perfectly with the Counselor's value system of wanting to help people.

The most important thing to remember as a Counselor is that your job is not to be a people pleaser. Instead, you are helping people by giving them what they need. This is what a trusted advisor does. You find out what your prospect's goals are, uncover the consequences of not taking action toward those goals, and hold your prospect's feet to the fire so that she will make the best decision to meet her goals.

OUT TO SEA

You've been through the sales cycle, and now you understand the advanced techniques that will help you become a top-producing Navigator in the long run. You are on your way and out to sea, selling the way people like to buy.

Chapter 10: Navigate the Tough Ones

But the most important part of *Navigate* isn't the strategies you use or the words you say. What makes *Navigate* truly powerful is your internal compass, and that's something only you can teach yourself to use to your greatest ability. In the last chapter, we'll show you why Navigating from the heart is the real make-or-break factor for your success in sales, and in life.

Chapter 11

NAVIGATE FROM THE HEART

A HEARTLESS NAVIGATOR LEARNS THE HARD WAY

A sales rep from our professional sales coaching division once held an Immediate Results workshop that was designed to sell tickets to one of Southwestern Consulting's large sales training conferences.

At the end of the rep's presentation, the general manager of the company he was presenting to stood up. "This looks great," he said. "I think we all like what you guys are offering, and it seems like everyone is interested in going. Here is my company credit card. Go ahead and sign us up for fifteen VIP tickets." Then the manager excused himself and headed off to his next meeting.

The rep was excited. Those fifteen VIP tickets amounted to a $6,000 order. He was writing up the sale when a couple of the other team members from the general manager's company approached him. "Actually, could you please give us seven tickets instead of fifteen?" they asked. "We're really concerned that fifteen tickets will break our budget."

The rep should have given them what they wanted. But seven tickets was less than half of the original sale. So instead, he just smiled and made the unfortunate decision to Navigate the situation in his favor.

He tracked down the general manager of the company, who was a Counselor. "Your team wanted to make sure they weren't being excessive with the decision to send fifteen people to the event, and I just want to make sure that you feel safe with that number," he said. "Your managers said that seven of them definitely want to attend, but I'm sure you have several team members who were not in attendance today whom you'd want to make sure we don't leave out. Would you like me to go ahead and throw two or three more tickets into this order to guarantee that we cover everyone who should be going?"

"Sure," the manager replied, "that sounds fine." And the rep happily rang up three *more* tickets than the team members agreed to.

But a week later, he received a call from that same general manager.

"You know, I thought the session you gave us was great, and my team was excited to go to your event," he said. "But when I talked to them afterward, they felt like they'd been taken advantage of. They said they asked you for seven tickets, and you went around them and sold me three more instead. We'd like to cancel our entire order."

The sad part of all this is that the sales rep in this story was me, Dustin.

I was the one leading the workshop that day. In fact, I was even supposed to be training one of our new sales reps in the *Navigate* system. What a great role model I turned out to be!

I felt so terrible about what I'd done that I didn't even know what to say to the general manager when I went back to his office to try to salvage the sale later. But the experience taught me a lesson I'll never forget. Always put your customers' best interests first. You should never sell to people just because you can. You should always identify the need first and then sell the way they want to buy.

You should always Navigate from the heart.

Chapter 11: Navigate from the Heart

THE HEART OF *NAVIGATE*

Understanding how to Navigate the different behavior styles is critical to reaching your full sales potential. But none of it is as important as the ultimate key to the *Navigate* system: Navigating from the heart.

You can follow every other strategy in this book, but none of them will matter if you leave this last one out. Navigating behavior styles is about connecting with people on a deeper emotional level. If your heart isn't in what you're doing, then that level of emotion simply doesn't exist. Unless you truly care about your clients and have the genuine desire to serve them, you will never make it as a Navigator. Your attempts to adapt to the different styles will come across as phony. And even if you manage to pull the wool over someone's eyes, that decision will come back to haunt you, just as it did for Dustin.

The ability to Navigate is a powerful skill. Selling the way people like to buy gives you the ability to connect with and influence them, for better or worse. With that power comes the responsibility to use it wisely.

As salespeople, we are trained to upsell our products and services, and with the tools *Navigate* gives you, you will have the skills to do that. These techniques will work on all different kinds of people, and the temptation will be there to manipulate them and take advantage of prospects who don't need or want your services. When that happens, you need to be able to depend on the internal compass of your heart to steer you straight again.

We talked in chapter 4 about the Platinum Rule, "treat others the way they want to be treated," and we said that, in sales, it is more effective than the Golden Rule. But in a much more important sense, the Golden Rule is really at the heart of the sales process after all.

We should always be as honest with and considerate of others as we want them to be with us. We should sell to people as though they are our fathers or mothers, our sons and daughters—as if they are us, ourselves. No one wants to be taken advantage of. When your heart is in the right place, your actions follow. And everybody benefits.

SERVICE AT HEART

The most powerful way to make sure your internal compass stays pointed to true north is to keep your heart focused on serving others.

When your focus is on closing the sale, you get "commission breath." You find yourself putting unhealthy pressure on both yourself and your prospect, and you tend to oversell. Your prospect sees dollar signs in your eyes, and a distance opens up between the two of you, like a canyon swallowing the trust that should be bringing you closer together. Your prospect's guard never comes down, and you lose the sale.

This is where the caricature of the "sleazy salesman" comes from. It's the result of too many salespeople focusing more on their own gain than on genuinely serving their clients. It's also the reason that so many people in sales call themselves "consultants" or "marketing professionals." They're ashamed to admit to their real job title because of the stigma attached to it.

But when you shift your focus to truly serving your prospects, that paradigm changes. You feel that success comes from the serving itself, rather than how much you sell. You learn that being a salesperson is really about giving, not getting, and that selling is not something you do *to* people, but something you do *for* them. You aim to provide value to your clients by asking them questions and really listening to the answers.

When you do this, a deeper connection with the people you're serving develops naturally. Your prospects understand that your honest intention is to help them, and that inspires them to take action in their own best interests. The byproduct of serving your

Chapter 11: Navigate from the Heart

clients like this is indeed more sales. But the sales aren't the focus of what you're doing. Instead, they're the fruit.

The "sleazy salesman" label that has haunted you your entire career disintegrates into thin air when you make the shift to serving others. In fact, you'll have good reason to consider selling one of the most honorable professions in the world. When someone asks what you do for a living, you won't dive for cover behind a fancy title anymore.

Instead, you'll look them square in the eyes and say, "I'm a salesperson, and I love it."

THE *NAVIGATE* EDGE

Becoming a Navigator gives you a competitive edge. But that edge isn't the one most outsiders think it is.

Top-producing Navigators draw their confidence from their intention to serve others, and from their work habits and acquired skills. They understand that the world of sales isn't about the results you see in a day, a week, or even a month. They know that when it comes to sales, the formula for success is service, practice, and consistency.

Champions aren't always the most talented people in a group. Rather, they're the people who put the most effort into their goals. They build their foundation on persistence and overcoming adversity whenever they face it.

As Theodore Roosevelt said, "The credit belongs to the man who is actually in the arena, whose face is marred by dust and sweat and blood . . . who knows great enthusiasms, the great devotions; who spends himself in a worthy cause; who at the best knows in the end the triumph of high achievement, and . . . if he fails, at least fails while daring greatly, so that his place shall never be with those cold and timid souls who neither know victory nor defeat."

When you put the hard work into becoming a true Navigator,

you gain an edge that no one can take away from you. It's not the price of your product. It's not the product itself.

Your edge is the ability to connect with others in a deep and meaningful way. And it will take you further than any other competitive edge in business.

THE ULTIMATE NAVIGATOR

Now that you're aware of the *Navigate* principles and techniques, you will never be bored again. You may already be itching to pick up the phone, walk through your office, or run over to the closest area that has the most people in it and start Navigating. You're looking forward to having fun reading people from afar while honing your skills, and to making that strong emotional connection with the people you serve—especially the ones who used to make no sense to you.

Wherever you go with *Navigate*, and whomever you meet along the way, keep your compass with you. Understand the shortcomings of the people around you, and learn to accept, love, and serve them anyway. When you can follow the Golden Rule and sell the way people like to buy at the same time, you have become a salesperson who truly navigates from the heart.

You have become the ultimate Navigator.

Enjoy the journey.

ACKNOWLEDGMENTS

We would like to acknowledge three groups of people who have helped to make this book possible.

The first group is our wives and kids. Without Kyah Hillis and Kristen Reiner holding down the forts at home and providing loving and caring support systems, we would not be able to work the way that we do.

Kyah: I love you more and more every day. Somehow you become even more beautiful each time I lay my eyes on you. I thank God every day that He gives you the grace and mercy to love a knucklehead like me. I love you.

Kristen: I know over the years you've put up with a lot you don't deserve from a prideful, self-centered, critical, results-oriented man. Your ongoing forgiveness and prayer have helped to transform me into a gentler, humbler spirit. I know I don't always tell you how much I appreciate your steadfast love, so let this be etched in stone: thank you for your incredible patience with me. I thank God every day for the unbelievable blessing He has provided me in you. I will always love you no matter what.

Without our kids, we would be much more self-centered than we already are. Haven Hillis and Kira, Anika, and Emma Reiner, you make life more fun and joyful for your fathers. Thank you for inspiring us, and thank you for being you!

The second group we'd like to acknowledge is our co-workers at Southwestern Consulting™. As of this writing, Southwestern Consulting™ has 115 team members, and without each and every

Acknowledgments

one of you doing what you do, we would not have been able to write this book.

To all the Southwestern Consulting™ sales and leadership coaches, thank you for being great examples and helping others reach their goals in life. To the Southwestern Consulting™ special ops team, thank you for your positive "can-do" attitudes and for helping to make sure that the wheels of our bus keep turning! To the Southwestern Consulting™ partners, thank you for living by the Southwestern Consulting™ Partners Pact and committing to being practitioners of everything you teach.

Last, and certainly not least, we are grateful to the Southwestern Consulting™ senior partners. Henry Bedford, Cindy Johnstone, Tim Nowak, Dave Brown, Emmie Brown, Gary Michels, Kitty Barrow, and Dan Moore—thank you for always having our backs. As we stumble and bumble through work and life, it's comforting to know we have a team of business partners we can count on when we need you the most.

The third group we'd like to acknowledge and thank is our editing and writing team.

Cindy Johnstone: Thank you for taking time out of your schedule to provide editing when we needed it. It is a blessing to have someone who is as scrupulously wise as you on our team! You are awesome!

Monica LaPlante: Thank you for your aesthetic creative marketing genius. You do an awesome job of making sure we look much cooler than we actually are.

Helen Chang, Kristine Serio, and the team at Author Bridge Media: Thank you for the amazing work you put into making *Navigate 2.0* come to life. We've loved working with you. Your attitude, work ethic, and diligence are much appreciated! We know that keeping us moving in the right direction is a full-time job, and you did it!

ABOUT THE AUTHORS

As the chief executive officer of Southwestern Family of Companies, **Dustin Hillis** is leading the organization toward its 30-year vision to become the largest privately owned company worldwide. Hillis plans to grow the company 26 percent each year to reach a total of 200 businesses by 2048. In addition to being CEO of Southwestern Family of Companies, Hillis remains in his role as the cofounder of Southwestern Consulting and head of Southwestern Coaching.

Hillis's career began while he was a student at the University of Tennessee – Knoxville. As a junior in college, Hillis became the all-time sales record holder at Southwestern Advantage, making a profit of more than $100,000 in just 14 weeks, and still holds the record to this day. As cofounder of Southwestern Consulting, Hillis oversees 200+ team members in locations including Estonia, the United Kingdom, Lithuania, Brazil, Canada, and all over the United States. The Southwestern Coaching business has a five-year compounded growth of 61 percent.

Hillis holds a degree in psychology and is a premier sales and leadership behavioral specialist. He is the author of the book *Navigate*, creator of the audio training series "How to Navigate a Referral System," and coauthor of the book *Speaking of Success* (with Stephen Covey, Ken Blanchard, and Jack Canfield). Hillis's next release will be a book titled *Redefining Possible* (coauthored with Ron Alford). Additionally, his insights on selling have been featured on some of the biggest podcasts in the world and in media outlets like *Entrepreneur* magazine and the *Dave Ramsey Show*.

About the Authors

Steve Reiner is a peak performance executive business and life coach as well as partner of the sales performance company Southwestern Consulting. Investing the last 30 years as a sales leader, he has consistently led by example, producing in the top 1 percent of salespeople. Reiner has recruited, trained, and managed more than 400 salespeople who have finished in the top 3 percent. His ability to equip people to be fearless, achieving breakthrough success in business and life, has been honed in more than 8,000 one-on-one sales and leadership consulting calls. Having personally knocked on more than 19,000 doors and conducted more than 12,000 presentations, Reiner knows how to get the most out of people, equipping them to be fearless, to crush their goals, and to have a blast doing it! His passion is helping people to remove the emotional hurdles that prevent them from excelling, taking them from a stressed-out state to one of "relaxed intensity." Having equipped thousands of people to multiply their earnings and their success in life, he not only helps them achieve breakthrough numbers but guides them through a process in which they can show up each day "in the zone"—prepared, without pressure, and fearless. Reiner lives in Colorado with his wife and three daughters.

TAKE YOUR BUSINESS TO THE NEXT LEVEL

Southwestern Consulting specializes in providing one-on-one accountability coaching for sales professionals and leaders. If you would like to talk with one of our certified consultants to help determine if we might be a fit for partnering with you, request a free call at http://FreeCall.TheNavigateBook.com